THE
MONON
BELL
RIVALRY

THE MONON BELL RIVALRY

CLASSIC CLASHES OF DEPAUW VS. WABASH

TYLER G. JAMES

THE
History
PRESS

Published by The History Press
Charleston, SC 29403
www.historypress.net

Copyright © 2013 by Tyler James
All rights reserved

Cover photo of Wabash's Ralph Lee Wilson (back row, far left) and team courtesy of
Crawfordsville District Public Library. Crowd photos of Wabash and DePauw fans courtesy
of Alex Turco.

First published 2013

ISBN 978.1.5402.3189.5

Library of Congress CIP data applied for.

To Ruth for listening, to Greg for pushing and to Mom and Dad for guiding the way.

CONTENTS

ACKNOWLEDGEMENTS

The following people have provided valuable work in making these pages come to life: Bill Wagner, DePauw sports information; Tom Runge, Wabash Alumni Affairs; Beth Swift, Lilly Library archivist; Wes Wilson, Roy O. West Library archivist; Christine DiGangi; Ellen Kobe; and Margaret Distler. Thank you.

INTRODUCTION

They can't even agree on what to call the game. For DePauw, it's Monon. For Wabash, it's The Bell Game. After 122 years of rivalry between the two schools, disagreements naturally form, even for the silliest reasons. The men of Wabash College, an all-male liberal arts school in Crawfordsville, Indiana, won't always agree with the student body at DePauw University, a coeducational liberal arts school twenty-eight miles south on U.S. Route 231 in Greencastle, Indiana. However, there will always be one agreement: the rivalry renewed annually in the officially-named Monon Bell Classic holds something special.

Matt Walker saw both sides of the rivalry as a young boy. Growing up in Crawfordsville as the son of a DePauw grad, he didn't have an allegiance to either school. One November he'd sit on the Wabash side, and the next he'd sit with DePauw.

"Even then, as a young pup not knowing a lot about what was going on, you still knew it was really different than anything else out there," said Walker, who ended up playing and coaching for DePauw. "I didn't know why, because I was a stupid, young kid. I didn't understand. But I could still tell. It was such an intense atmosphere it almost scared me as a young kid. You knew it was special then."

The rivalry has been developed around differences—perceived, created or legitimate—between two fundamentally similar institutions. At DePauw, they are Tigers, wearing old gold and black. At Wabash, they are Little Giants, colored with scarlet and white. Methodists founded the school in

Greencastle. Presbyterians created the institution in Crawfordsville. Wabash calls its rivals Dannies, painting a picture of snooty, rich kids who haven't worked a day in their lives. At DePauw, Wabash students are known as Wallies, cavemen creatures grunting in classrooms without women. Even athletic slogans show a split. The Little Giants had "Wabash Always Fights," so DePauw countered with "DePauw Never Quits."

Some players learned to embrace the rivalry during the recruiting process. Phil Eskew's mother wouldn't let him go to an all-male Wabash. Jason Geringer took pride in telling the Wabash coaches that he picked DePauw. He's missed only one Monon Bell, because of the birth of his first child, since graduating in 2002. "I said, 'I made up my mind to go to DePauw,' and the Wabash coach on the phone said, 'Well Jason, tell me what made that decision.' I told him, 'Coach, honestly I decided I wanted to go to school with girls.' And he said, 'Jason, you mean to tell me you're passing up a quality education just so you can chase tail in biology class?' And I said, 'Coach, if it's a choice between chasing tail or not chasing tail, my decision is made.'"

Dave Husted learned his distaste for DePauw soon after enrolling at Wabash. "It was just sort of a given that everybody there disliked DePauw," said Husted. "It was one of those things that was sort of drilled into everybody from the beginning. The Dannies were pictured as a little arrogant, carrying umbrellas wherever they went and having all the girlfriends."

For the same reasons DePauw students slight Wabash, those connected to the Crawfordsville college embrace the tradition of the school. Former head coach Chris Creighton spent seven years at Wabash, leaving with a stronger connection to the school than he has to his own alma mater:

I feel more a part of Wabash than I do Kenyon, my alma mater. I love Kenyon, but I'm a wannabe alum of Wabash. Wabash College is special. What they do for young men is unlike any place I've ever heard of. They take motivated and bright young men and challenge them in ways that they've never been challenged before and basically take these bright, motivated, studly guys to the brink of where I don't know if I can do this. They're pushed and challenged to do things that they'd never done before and maybe don't think are possible. And…they're supported in unbelievable ways to actually achieve those challenges. Then these guys are the most confident group of people that I've ever been around. They know that they can go out and make a difference in the world and that there isn't a challenge that they can't overcome. Wabash fundamentally changes its students in that way, and it's awesome.

Such passion for a school carries the Monon Bell rivalry through all twelve months of the year. By the time November rolls around, the two schools are ready to fight on (and sometimes off) the field. The opposing crowds are now separated after scuffles between fans escalated in the 1990s. On at least one occasion, the referees made the teams attempt an extra point on the other side of the field from where the touchdown was scored because of a scrum leaking into the end zone.

Those most passionate about the Monon Bell Classic have their own connection to one of the schools. For me, it's the school in Greencastle. I first encountered the rivalry as a freshman football player at DePauw in 2007. That game ended with a game-winning field goal as time expired, and I've been hooked since Jordan Havercamp's kick sailed through the uprights for a Tigers victory. Knee injuries cut my career short before I could step onto the playing field for a Monon Bell Classic, but my sideline experience sucked me in. The rest of my college career was spent working for *The DePauw*, the university's student-run newspaper. When a scarlet "W" was spray-painted on a DePauw campus landmark in the fall of 2009, I carried on the time-honored tradition of ripping the opposing school in print. The Tigers haven't won a Monon Bell game since that column was published.

The passion of the rivalry, whether expressed through words, vandalism or even thievery, matches anything I've ever encountered in my short career as a sports journalist. The stories I've learned while researching this book only reinforced my previous thoughts. Former Wabash quarterback Dave Knott likes to use former Wabash president Andy Ford as the epitome of passion for the rivalry. After Knott's son, Jake, threw a game-winning touchdown pass in 2001 to end a five-year losing streak to DePauw, Ford invited Dave Knott and others to celebrate at his home late into the night. Knott couldn't find anyone happier about the outcome than Ford. "He just hated DePauw, and it just killed him when they beat us every year," Knott said. "But yet he wanted football to take its proper place. He wanted to win, but he wanted to win within a set rules. He had the perfect mentality."

The following year, Wabash routed DePauw in Crawfordsville. At halftime, the Little Giants led 35–0, and a final victory in the regular season before a trip to the playoffs seemed all but assured. But there was Ford, urging the Wabash team for more.

"I'm thinking if I'm the coach, I'm not going to take a chance that any of my better players are getting hurt because I'm playing again next week," Knott said. "And there's the president leaning over that balcony with the veins popping out of his head screaming at the players to put thirty-five more on them in the second half. He's yelling at them, 'Let's beat them by seventy.' He wants thirty-five more."

The total wins and losses between both schools have remained close for more than a century. Wabash leads the series with a 57–53–9 record and holds a 38–37–6 advantage since the introduction of the rivalry's trophy.

The memories of Monon Bell victories and defeats rest in the minds of every player to put on a Wabash or DePauw jersey. The victories are always cherished, but sometimes the defeats weigh more. A career-ending loss to the rival can scar and keep former players from attending games at the opposing team's field for years. Perspective wins out before long. The results of a Division III football rivalry don't carry with former players into their jobs away from the sport after graduation.

"Colleges like Wabash and DePauw are both fine colleges where athletics were important as a part of the rounded education, but this is not Division I football. This is not where people don't graduate," said former Wabash player Allan Anderson. "This is where people go to go to medical school, to go to law school. I think we had a different perspective on athletics as part of our college lives. Were we disappointed? Was I personally disappointed? Absolutely. But you're young."

Anderson finished his career at Wabash in 1964 without a single victory over DePauw. He remembers head coach Ken Keuffel checking in his players late one night after another Monon Bell loss. "He came over because he was worried about his boys," Anderson said. "Well, we had forgotten about it. Not because we had too many beers; we had plenty of beers, but we had forgotten about it because we were kids and it wasn't the only thing in our lives. Now do we remember it? Sure we remember it, but it's a fond memory."

Those fond memories litter the pages that follow. More memorable moments will come for DePauw and Wabash with every clang of the Monon Bell.

Chapter 1

1932-34: THE BEGINNINGS OF THE BELL

The Monon Bell started as a gift. DePauw University and Wabash College have been fighting over it ever since.

In November 1932, the Monon Railroad, which in part connected the two Indiana campuses in Greencastle and Crawfordsville, donated a three-hundred-pound locomotive bell from one of its steam-engine trains to award to the winner of the annual football game between the two schools. The Monon Railroad's desire to be connected to the annual game made sense, as it had branded itself as a reliable transportation to five major schools in the state: DePauw, Wabash, Purdue, Indiana and Butler. The railroad even borrowed the school colors from Wabash and DePauw for their trains—red and gray for its passenger cars and black and gold for its freight engines.

The football rivalry between both schools already featured thirty-eight games in forty-two years. Wabash won nineteen games, DePauw won sixteen and the two teams tied three times before the new trophy was introduced. The annual football games created a rivalry between the two schools, but so did the makeup of their student body. Both based their education in the liberal arts, but a fundamental difference between the two schools was formed in the previous century. Wabash, founded in 1832 by Presbyterian ministers, remained an all-male institution. DePauw, founded as Indiana Asbury University in 1837 by the Methodist Church, started admitting women as early as 1867. The name change, a dedication to donor Washington C. DePauw, came in 1884.

So when the Monon Railroad handed over one if its locomotive bells, it became a part of a rivalry steeped in tradition. The idea of a trophy for the football rivalry was first publicly suggested by 1925 DePauw graduate Orien Fifer in a letter to the editor sent to the *Indianapolis News*. Later that year, the Monon Bell, first described as the victory bell, made its debut at a DePauw pep session the day before the 1932 matchup. DePauw publicity director Russell Alexander presented the trophy, with its chassis painted red and the bell painted gold, to fans gathered on the Greencastle campus.

For the first time, the winner of the clash between the Little Giants of Wabash and the Tigers of DePauw would take home more than just pride.

SOON AFTER INTERCOLLEGIATE FOOTBALL started being played in Indiana, the rivalry between Wabash and DePauw was born. Fittingly, both schools might not agree on who played a football game first.

On October 25, 1884, a Wabash team led by coach Ed Taber headed southeast to play a game against Butler University at Indianapolis Baseball Park. Winning by a 4–0 score with the help of four field goals from Jesse Tabor, Wabash claimed a victory in what the school claims as the first intercollegiate football game played in Indiana.

DePauw records also show a game of its own against Butler in 1884. Listed as a May 31 matchup, DPU was shut out against the Christian school from Indianapolis while allowing four touchdowns. Regardless of who played the first game, Wabash went on to play the first multi-game season of either school. In 1886, the school from Crawfordsville compiled a 2–0–1 record under coach Evans Woolen and claimed the first state championship in Indiana with wins over Franklin College and Hanover College and a tie against Franklin.

Four years later, DePauw and Wabash squared off for the first time. Separated by twenty-eight miles, the two schools became instant rivals. A 34–5 victory for DePauw in 1890 marked the first of seven straight annual meetings between the two. Making up for lost time during a three-year hiatus, DePauw and Wabash played each other twice in both 1900 and 1901.

In 1903, the two schools faced a conflict bigger than the sport. After traveling to Crawfordsville, the DePauw team refused to leave the locker room upon hearing that the Wabash lineup included African American player Sam Gordon. Wabash legend says Lew Wallace, a former general in the Civil War who lived a successful career as a politician and novelist, including writing *Ben Hur: A Tale of Christ*, played a role in coaxing the DePauw team to play. Wallace, living in Crawfordsville at the time, helped Methodist

A head injury in a game against St. Louis University led to the death of Wabash player Ralph "Sap" Wilson in 1910. Before passing away, Wilson's last words were, "Did Wabash win?" The Little Giants won 10–0, but Wilson's death led to the remainder of the season being cancelled. *Courtesy of Crawfordsville District Public Library.*

ministers from DePauw convince the team to take the field. Wabash won the game by a 14–0 score, but the teams didn't play the following year because Wabash used another African American player, William Cantrell.

Wabash continued strong play through the rest of the decade. In 1904, the team was given the nickname of the Little Giants by a newspaper reporter for its competitive play against schools much larger than itself. The following year, the newly named Little Giants defeated the University of Notre Dame 5–0 in South Bend. The storied Fighting Irish won their first national championship (1924) before losing a home game again (1928). The 1905 win marked the only triumph Wabash would have against Notre Dame in eleven matchups. The University of Michigan even travelled to play against Wabash in 1907. One of two losses for the Little Giants that season, Michigan defeated Wabash 22–0 at Washington Park in Indianapolis.

In 1910, the DePauw-Wabash rivalry was interrupted for the last time. The Little Giants played four games to start the season, accumulating a 4–0 record and a 118–0 aggregate advantage. But in the fourth game, freshman Ralph "Sap" Wilson suffered a head injury. Tackling a St. Louis University ball carrier, Wilson took a knee to his skull. Hours after the game, Wilson died as the result of a skull fracture. His last words: "Did Wabash win?" The quote remains engraved on his tombstone in Crawfordsville's Oak Hill cemetery and has become apart of Wabash football lore.

The rest of the 1910 season was cancelled, wiping out the game against the Greencastle foes. The rivalry was renewed in 1911 and has remained an annual tradition in every year that's followed.

WITH THE MONON BELL up for grabs for the first time, an added excitement surrounded the 1932 matchup between DePauw and Wabash. The *Indianapolis News* featured daily stories on the upcoming game, but by midweek, snowstorms hit Greencastle. On Wednesday and Thursday, DePauw's athletic director employed a small army of workers to remove eight inches of snow from the Blackstock Field playing surface in preparation for Saturday's game. One *News* story jabbed DePauw president G. Bromley Oxnam, a University of Southern California alum, for not knowing how to handle snow.

Up in Crawfordsville, Wabash head coach Pete Vaughan had ten inches of his own snow to deal with. Practices were held indoors all week long until Thursday night, when his team trudged through several inches of snow remaining on Ingalls Field.

The game would be the last in the lauded career of DePauw halfback Don Wheaton. The local Greencastle newspaper, the *Daily Banner*, called Wheaton "one of the greatest halfbacks ever produced at DePauw." Wheaton led the Tigers to victories in 1930 and 1931 as a part of all three touchdowns scored in both games. In '30, a Wheaton touchdown pass to Forrest Crain set up an extra-point score for Wheaton in a 7–6 DePauw victory. Wheaton followed the previous year's performance with two touchdowns—one on the ground in the third quarter and one by air on a pass to Robert Bradley in the fourth quarter—for a 13–7 win in '31.

Following his junior season on a 7–1 DePauw team, Wheaton was named an all-state performer by the *Indianapolis Star* and an honorable mention all-American by multiple press outlets. Famed sportswriter Grantland Rice placed Wheaton on his third-team all-American squad. The 1932 campaign served as Wheaton's victory lap, but the season didn't progress as well as the

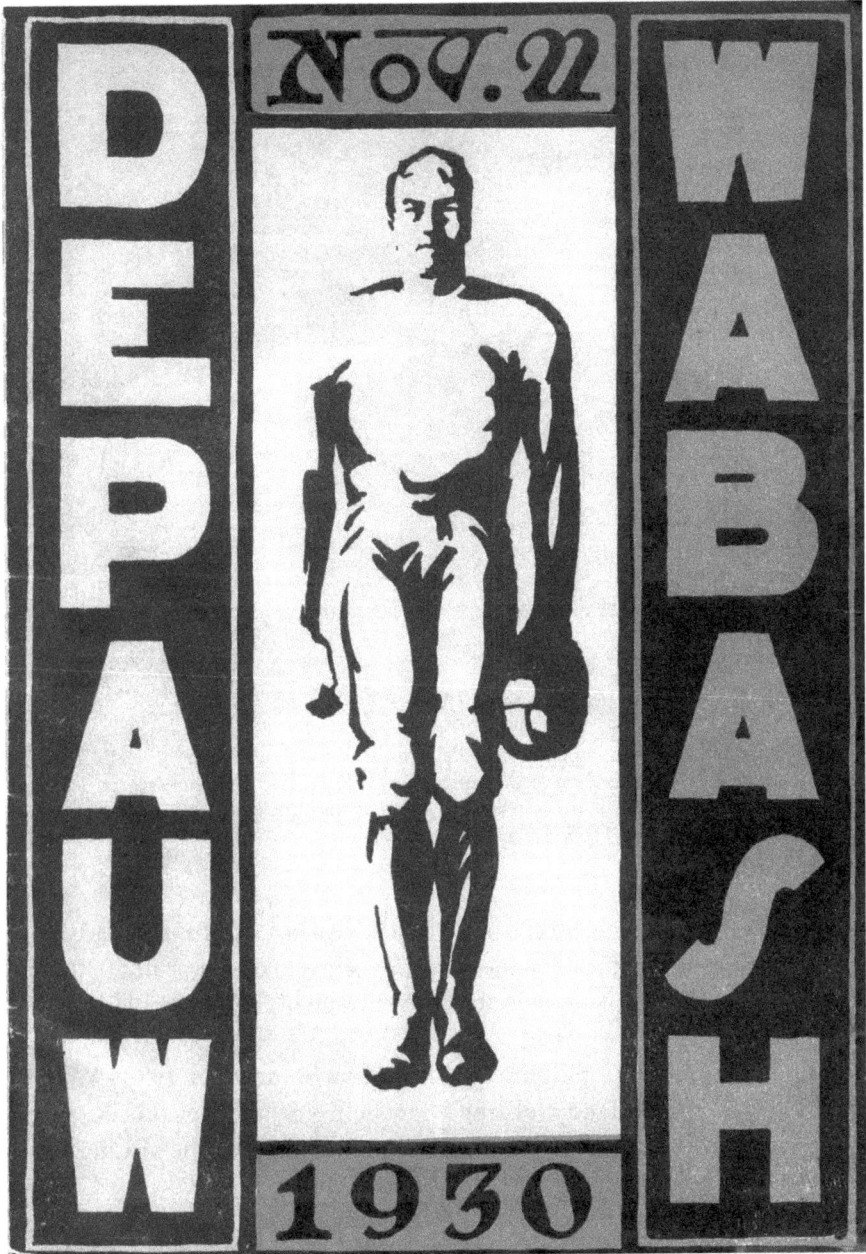

Game program for the 1930 matchup between DePauw and Wabash at Blackstock Field.
Courtesy of DePauw Archives.

Gaumey Neal brought winning ways to DePauw as head coach from 1930 to 1945. Neal's 1933 squad finished with the best record in DePauw history. The '33 Tigers scored 136 points and allowed 0 points in a 7–0 season that ended with the first win in a game played for the Monon Bell trophy. *Courtesy of DePauw Archives.*

previous two. DePauw head coach Gaumey Neal, a Wabash graduate, faced multiple losses in a season for the first time since taking over in 1930. The Tigers needed a victory over Wabash to salvage a .500 record after a 3–4 start to the season.

Poor playing conditions limited Wheaton on Saturday. A 4–2–1 Wabash squad prepared to defend DePauw's backfield star and welcomed any aid in slowing down Wheaton. A scoreless first half favored the visiting Little Giants. A seven-man front line of Charles Wrona, Irvin Powers, Gordon Stierwalt, Robert Mueller, Donald Reinert, Earl Peterson and Gary Vinroot held strong despite playing without injured center and captain Heman Powers.

The second half brought scoring opportunities for both sides. In the third quarter, Wabash's offense drove as deep into Tiger territory as the twelve-yard line but surrendered the ball on downs. DePauw received its best scoring chance so far in the third quarter when Alvin Volkman blocked a punt to give his offense the ball at the Wabash thirty-yard line. On the ensuing drive, Wheaton completed a pass to Robert Fribley that moved the ball to the five-yard line, but Wheaton fumbled shortly after to kill the scoring chance.

Stuart Smith, starting quarterback for the 1932 Wabash team, wrote about his memories from the '32 game for a Wabash publication celebrating the 100th game in 1993. He provided a vivid memory of one missed scoring chance. "We lined up, and I barked the signals: 976...84...32...51...hike! The 8 meant that we would shift to the right...the 4 indicated the trailing halfback would carry the ball, and he would hit the #3 hole between their left guard and tackle," Smith wrote. "Our line had DePauw kissing the ground. One could have driven a freight train through that hole. The result...our trailing half, Red Varner, slipped and fell on the four-yard line."

Two more DePauw attacks at the goal line were stopped by Wabash in the fourth quarter. Wheaton was taken down at the three-yard line to end one drive, and a twenty-five-yard pass attempt to Bradley in the end zone sailed out of reach in the final minute. The first DePauw-Wabash game played for the Monon Bell ended in a 0–0 tie. Winners of the '31 matchup, DePauw kept the bell in Greencastle.

THE DEPAUW TIGERS could do no wrong in 1933. The closest game of the season came in the opener, when the Tigers defeated Ball State by a 9–0 margin. The lone touchdown of the game came from DePauw center George Lortz, who picked up a blocked punt and scrambled ninety-nine yards for a score. A dominating defense was just getting started for the '33 "Old Gold" squad. Confidence ran so high in Greencastle that the *Daily Banner* sent out a warning to Wabash in a story recapping the season opener.

Each week, teams would line up across from the DePauw eleven and be denied access to the end zone. And as if trying to rectify the 0–0 tie with Wabash that ended the '32 season, the offense started to roll over opponents as well. The scores piled up:

DePauw 28, Earlham 0
DePauw 13, Manchester 0
DePauw 12, Hanover 0
DePauw 26, Franklin 0
DePauw 34, Evansville 0

The 1933 DePauw football team finished its season with an unbeaten, untied and unscored-upon record. *Courtesy of DePauw Archives.*

By the time DePauw's annual battle with Wabash rolled around in late November, the Tigers remained undefeated, untied and unscored upon with a 122–0 aggregate. The only foe to have any luck in Greencastle was runaway bank-robber John Dillinger. He and his legendary crew walked away with $74,782.09 from the Central National Bank on Monday, October 23.

DePauw head coach Gaumey Neal packed up his team to return to his alma mater in Crawfordsville for the new tradition of the Monon Bell battle. A crowd of more than two thousand gathered at Wabash to see if the local Little Giants could upend the perfect Tigers. After one half, the crowd may have assumed the home team would do just that. Wabash racked up nine first downs before halftime, while the DePauw offense struggled to manage only two of its own. But the Tigers had given up yards before. It was points that were hard to come by.

In the second half, DePauw's offense ignited a rally. Halfback Robert Bradley ripped off a run of thirty yards and followed that with a forty-yard

completion to Alvin Volkman. Three tries from the eight-yard line were denied, but Bradley found fullback Earl Pierce for a touchdown reception on fourth down. A Bradley extra point gave DePauw a 7–0 lead.

As to be expected, the Old Gold defense didn't need any more help. Regardless, the Tigers added seven more points for punctuation on an unprecedented season for the school. A two-yard Pierce touchdown run and Bradley extra point pushed the final score to 14–0 in favor of the Tigers.

The numbers added up for a memorable DePauw campaign: 136 points scored, 0 points allowed, seven wins, zero losses, zero ties and one Monon Bell.

PETE VAUGHAN KNEW how to win at Wabash. Throughout the 1920s, Vaughan's Scarlet teams rolled over DePauw almost every year. The Little Giants won eight of the ten meetings in the decade, including seven straight

Wabash head coach Robert E. Vaughan, known as Pete, started his tenure in 1919, more than a decade before the Monon Bell was introduced to the rivalry with DePauw, and compiled 115 wins by the time he ended his career following the 1945 season. *Courtesy of DePauw Archives.*

from 1921 to 1927. The first six in the winning streak came in dominating fashion. Wabash won those games by a combined 118 points while holding DePauw scoreless in each game.

DePauw's hiring of Wabash graduate Gaumey Neal to be its head coach proved troubling for Vaughan. Neal, who had played as a senior in Vaughan's first year as a head coach in 1919, made an immediate impact on the Greencastle side of the rivalry. In his first four tries, he led DePauw to three wins and one tie. His team continued to roll in the 1934 season.

The winning ways of 1933 transferred into the following season despite losing eight regular contributors to graduation. Seven wins to start the 1934 campaign extended the DePauw unbeaten streak to sixteen and winning streak to fourteen. The Tigers hadn't lost a football game since before the Monon Bell was introduced in 1932. The DePauw defense remained stout in '34 as well. Continuing the dominant '33 season, the Old Gold defenders didn't allow a touchdown until a game against Georgetown College in the first week of November.

As had become tradition, the final game in November against Wabash would still test DePauw's true excellence. The Little Giants took to Greencastle with a middling 3–2–2 record. Since a 41–0 loss to Washington University–St. Louis in October, the Scarlet eleven rebounded with two ties sandwiched between two wins.

With unseasonably nice weather greeting fans at Blackstock Field, attendance of nearly five thousand was reported from the game. A slow first quarter didn't provide much to cheer about, but action picked up in the second stanza. Wabash's C. Dale Riggs recovered a fumble by DePauw halfback Robert Fribley at the DPU forty-seven-yard line to flip field position. The Little Giants punted the ball back, but possession remained in Old Gold territory for most of the quarter. The Scarlet offense put its best drive together following a Fribley punt out to his own forty-six-yard line. Wabash halfback Herm Berns tracked a twenty-two-yard gain with a run over the right end. The drive appeared to stall after losing yardage on the next three plays, but a fourth-down heave put the Little Giants ahead. Berns started with the ball right and faded backward with nowhere to go. He tossed the ball downfield, where William "Booie" Snyder caught the pigskin at the ten-yard line. Avoiding two defenders, Snyder ran into the end zone for the go-ahead score. An extra-point kick from Paul Mueller gave Wabash the 7–0 lead it would take into halftime.

A scoreless third quarter led into an action-filled fourth quarter. Early in the period, DePauw seemed poised to score its first points of the game. A pass from Fribley to Earl Pierce moved the Tiger offense to the Wabash thirty-two-yard line. Another Fribley pass, this time to William Kinnally, advanced the pigskin to the twenty-yard line. Wabash's Snyder broke up a pass in the end zone, but the ball wouldn't reach the goal line again in the drive for DePauw. The Scarlet defense forced a turnover on downs at the ten-yard line.

An Old Gold threat returned quickly. Riggs fumbled the ball for Wabash, and DePauw's William Horst recovered it at the sixteen. Three rushes by Jerome Schilling, Fribley and Homer Bishop moved the offense inside the one-yard line, but a fourth-down miscue resulted in an eleven-yard loss for Schilling, and Wabash regained possession.

One last surge remained for DePauw late in the fourth quarter. A drive that started at the Wabash forty-four-yard line progressed to the twenty-four on a pass from Schilling to Wendell Kay. A Fribley run to the fourteen and reception to the four set up an eventual touchdown run off the right tackle for the senior halfback. Trailing by a point, the Tigers ran the same play for the extra-point attempt, but the Little Giant defense stood tall.

Clinging to a 7–6 lead, Wabash almost saw the victory slip away. Berns returned the ensuing kickoff to the twenty-nine-yard line, but the ball squirted away from him as he went to the ground. A DePauw player landed on the loose ball, but Berns was ruled down before losing possession. The

Above: DePauw head coach Gaumey Neal talks with Bob Johnson (53) and Bob Steuber (37) in 1943. Both players joined the Tigers for the season while assigned to DePauw for naval training. Johnson previously played at Purdue, and Steuber had played at Missouri before being drafted by the Chicago Bears in April 1943. Steuber joined DePauw shortly after playing an NFL game against the Green Bay Packers. He tallied 266 yards and 25 points in the 1943 Monon Bell Classic, a 33–0 DePauw victory. *Courtesy of DePauw Archives.*

Opposite, top: Game action from the 1938 Monon Bell Classic in Greencastle. DePauw won the game 7–0. *Courtesy of DePauw Archives.*

Opposite, bottom: Game action from the 1939 Monon Bell Classic in Crawfordsville. DePauw won the game 7–0. *Courtesy of DePauw Archives.*

Game program for the 1943 Monon Bell Classic at Blackstock Stadium. *Courtesy of DePauw Archives.*

Former head coach Gaumey Neal was greeted warmly at DePauw decades after his 1933 team finished a perfect season. *Courtesy of DePauw Archives.*

Little Giants held onto the ball and the victory. For the first time, the scarlet and white were able to ring the Monon Bell.

Just two years after it was introduced as the official trophy of the DePauw-Wabash rivalry, both teams had earned possession with a victory. Each school would learn to yearn for the clang of an old railroad bell.

Chapter 2

1955: THE KICK TO END THE DROUGHT

DEPAUW 23, WABASH 20

The Monon Bell rivalry turned bleak for DePauw in the early 1950s. In the midst of a six-year losing streak to Wabash, the football program in Greencastle hit near rock bottom. The 1952 loss to the Little Giants, a 47–0 shellacking, marked the worst DePauw defeat against Wabash since the Monon Bell was introduced in 1932. The loss sent DePauw into a tailspin for the next two seasons.

The Tigers went through their entire eight-game schedule in 1953 scoring fewer points (44) than Wabash scored against them in the '52 finale. A 0–7–1 season ended with another dismantling at the hands of the Little Giants by a 41–0 score. The 1954 DePauw squad doubled its scoring output from the previous season but matched its winless record. The Tigers once again ended a 0–7–1 season with a loss to Wabash, this time by a 28–0 margin.

"There was a little bit of a defeatist attitude when I came in there as a freshman," said Morrie Goodnight, who arrived on campus in the fall of '54. "All of us on the freshman team thought we have to change this. We scrimmaged the varsity all the time and beat them a few times. We knew things were going to get better."

The shakeup took full of effect following the '54 season. No wins in two full seasons and a 116–0 aggregate in three games against rival Wabash didn't qualify as acceptable. With the support of new athletic director James Loveless, a 1929 graduate and three-time letter-winner in both football and basketball, DePauw head coach Mike Snavely hit the recruiting trail hard to bring in better athletes with higher expectations. Two of the biggest targets became Tom Campbell and Dwight Tallman.

"Doctor Loveless came in at about that time, and he was more energetic about the program," Campbell said. "He solicited the help of previous players and alumni more strenuously than I think had ever been done before. My experience was the result of a fellow who was an alum of the university in my hometown. He's really the person who got me started looking at DePauw."

Campbell, an Indiana All-Star and all-American from Sullivan, Indiana, weighed his options, which included a couple Big Ten programs, but chose DePauw with the aid of a full-ride academic scholarship from General Motors. While on a visit to Purdue, Campbell met all-star tackle Dwight Tallman from New Castle, Indiana, who also ended up at DePauw. "He and I both stood up on the press box of Purdue University and watched them play Ohio State," Campbell said. "We were side by side and had just met each other then and then ended up at DePauw together."

The DePauw starting lineup included Campbell for the '55 season opener in September. The only freshman starter, Campbell joined a trio of seniors in the Tiger backfield. Dick McCracken, back from two years studying in England, took the starting quarterback spot, while Fred Williams claimed the starting fullback position after an injury-riddled junior season. Art Bryant, a five-foot-ten, 155-pound speedster, returned as a halfback following a junior campaign as the team's MVP.

After a season-opening, 39–7 loss to University of Evansville, Mike Snavely didn't hesitate to tinker with his lineup. In the second game, Skip Mathieson replaced Williams as the starting fullback. Mathieson had waited a year for a chance to play at DePauw since transferring from Brown University. A self-described Pennsylvania coal miner, Mathieson found he didn't fit in at Brown as a freshman. Looking for an opportunity to play college football, the Sharon High School graduate heard about DePauw from Loveless, who was leaving his coaching post at nearby Grove City College in western Pennsylvania to return to his alma mater. Loveless convinced Mathieson to follow him to Greencastle in '54.

Sophomore quarterback Morrie Goodnight, who had also been waiting for his chance to play at DePauw, helped provide an offensive spark in the second game. DePauw was unable to come back in the home opener against St. Joseph's College, but Goodnight, inserted into the lineup in the second quarter, accounted for both Tiger scores with a rushing and a passing touchdown in a 27–13 defeat.

Still, the winning ways were missing for DePauw. Even a local newspaper had fun with the DePauw winless streak. Playing with the title of the 1955 Spencer Tracy film *Bad Day at Black Rock*, one headline read "Another Bad Day in Blackstock."

The new blood in the program wasn't willing to accept the mediocrity. In the third game of the season, Ball State University came to Blackstock Stadium to play the Tigers in an Indiana Collegiate Conference matchup. The thought of starting the season 0–3 seemed dishonorable.

"The atmosphere we found in the first couple games in the locker room was not a winning atmosphere," Campbell said. "We had seniors who goofed off and jacked around before games. They weren't serious. Before the Ball State game, Dwight Tallman took a senior tackle and threw him out the back door of the stadium because he was goofing off. That just sort of set the tone for that Ball State game, and we went out and won."

Tallman, a six-foot-five, 215-pound freshman tackle, had played in only a reserve role but represented the feelings of many players dedicated to the program. That afternoon, Morrie Goodnight earned the first start of his career, and the Tigers jumped out to a 7–0 lead after the first half. A seventy-one-yard touchdown run by Bryant gave DePauw its first lead of the season. Another Bryant touchdown in the second half, followed by a blocked punt recovered in the end zone by Tom Holthouse, gave DePauw a 19–6 victory over Ball State.

"These were freshmen who were kicking seniors' rear ends. The atmosphere changed almost 180 degrees when this group of freshmen came in," Campbell said. "That's not taking anything away from Morrie or Skip or Art. The atmosphere was just different, and it promoted their playing ability. Then they took off, and it all came together."

With the youth infusion, the DePauw offense started rolling. The Tigers scored 41 and 40 points in consecutive wins against Oberlin College and Valparaiso University, respectively. The Tigers reached a 3–2 record and led the ICC in rushing yardage with 230 per game. Bryant led the attack with over 8 yards per carry and five touchdowns. DePauw's winning streak ended at three games when Butler University delivered an 18–7 defeat on October 22. The following week, DePauw took down undefeated Beloit College, which entered the game 6–0, and all of a sudden, the campus started thinking positively about the Monon Bell matchup two weeks in advance.

"As that year built to the game, it became more exciting. We certainly knew we had a chance to break a tradition," Mathieson said. "It became an exciting thing for us to look forward as the season kept going along and we kept getting our share of the wins. We felt like we had a chance to win."

"I'd suit up if the Coach would let me, hang it!"

BEAT
WABASH

AND "BEAT" IT DOWN TO
PROGRESSIVE PRINTING COMPANY TO BUY
YOUR CHRISTMAS CARDS TODAY!

A local business joined in supporting DePauw for the 1952 Monon Bell Classic with a newspaper advertisement. *Courtesy of DePauw Archives.*

While confidence was growing within the team, particular praise came from Jerry Pontius, sports editor for *The DePauw*. Pontius buried a wager at the end of his regular "Sideline Supporter" column. On November 2, he wrote, "Incidentally—and you'll notice I insert this in the final paragraph, hoping few people will see it—yours truly, as a final gesture, will ring the cherished Monon Bell for one hour if the Tigers come out on the long end of the score Nov. 12th. See you then."

DePAUW WOULD NEED more than a partial season's momentum to beat Wabash and end the six-game Monon Bell losing streak. The series advantage had never been tilted in one team's favor more than it had after the '54 victory for Wabash. A 32–24–5 series record gave the Little Giants an eight-game advantage. The '55 Wabash squad showed no signs of letting the DePauw losing streak come to a close.

Wabash entered the game with a 5–2–1 record under a makeshift coaching staff. Head coach Garland Frazier was hospitalized for an appendectomy during the latter half of the season, and line coach Walt Bartkiewicz filled Frazier's role in his absence. The Little Giants didn't share a conference with the Tigers, but both teams compiled a 2–1 record against common opponents. Both teams beat Valparaiso and split games against Beloit and Butler. DePauw's loss came to Butler, which Wabash had beaten 14–12 the week before the Monon Bell game, back in October. Wabash's 19–13 loss to Beloit in early October was bested by DePauw's victory over the undefeated team in the season's seventh week.

The focus on the Wabash campus remained even-keeled. Senior Bob Schwab said the team refused to let overconfidence prevail in Crawfordsville. "You really didn't think about that sort of thing. The guys that did that kind of thinking were the cheerleaders saying 'Beat the Dannies,'" Schwab said. "We were too wrapped up in the strategy of what was going to happen."

Meanwhile in Greencastle, the frustration had been building in a senior class that hadn't been able to ring the Bell. Guys like Jerry Rose, who started at center on the '55 team, grew to understand the dislike for the rival school of Wabash. "Some of it just came from the football team because this was our prime opponent, the nearest team to us geographically and the history of the rivalry," Rose said. "It was Wabash men versus DePauw men and women. So we always thought we had something more going than they did—a broader view on life. There's a lot of rivalry that people who were playing football felt because it was carried on from one class to the next. The coach, Mike Snavely, had a lot to do with it. He used to throw down the gauntlet to a challenge."

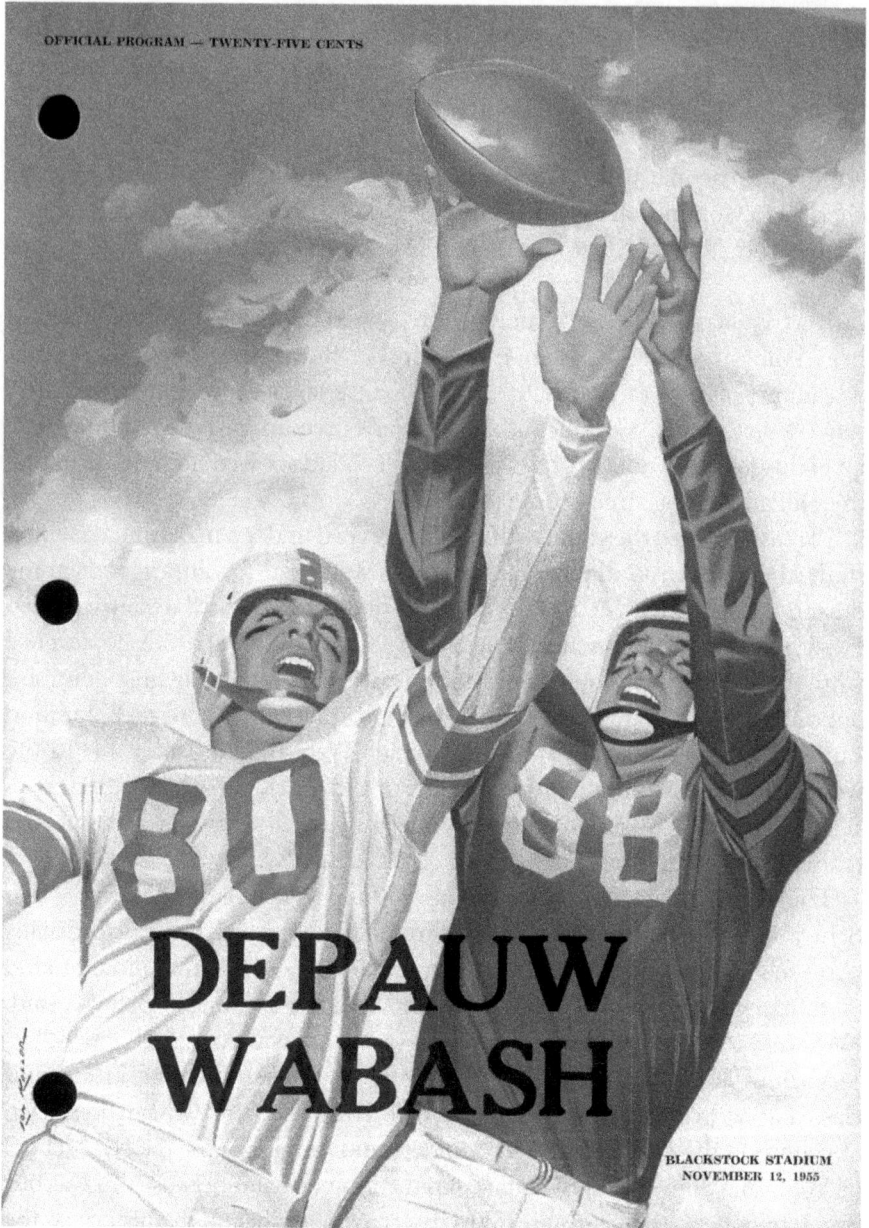

Game program for the 1955 Monon Bell Classic at Blackstock Stadium. *Courtesy of DePauw Archives.*

The sixty-first matchup between DePauw and Wabash ended up being the last challenge for Snavely and seniors like halfback Art Bryant. "We were hungry. But even if we had just lost one year, there would be a lot of motivation," Bryant said. "It was getting kinda embarrassing when you lose six in a row."

DEPAUW STARTED THE FIRST HALF like a team desperate to ring the Monon Bell. Overhead, a plane flew above Blackstock Stadium with a banner reading "Go Wabash, Beat DePauw." Playing on their home turf, the Tigers had a different idea.

Quarterback Morrie Goodnight engineered the first scoring drive of the game eight minutes into the first quarter. Starting at the DePauw thirty-two-yard line, the drive showed promise after a forty-four-yard pass from Goodnight to halfback Art Bryant. Goodnight capped the drive with a two-yard touchdown run. The home-team Tigers led 6–0 following a missed extra point by Fred Williams.

The Tigers added to their lead in the second quarter with more strong play from Goodnight and Bryant. This time DePauw drove ninety-four yards on fifteen plays for the second score of the game. A twenty-yard reception by Bryant highlighted a drive that ended with a twelve-yard Bryant touchdown run. The combination of timely passes to counter a strong running attack kept the Wabash defense off balance. The twenty-yard reception came on a particular favorite play of Bryant's. "We worked on it. It was kind of one of our favorite plays," Bryant said. "I went through the line and cut across the middle, and he hit me." The play-action passes were run off a belly series in which Goodnight would read the defense before deciding which of his options to follow through with. The ball often ended up in the hands of fullback Skip Mathieson or halfbacks Tom Campbell and Bryant.

An offensive line composed of Jerry Rose at center, Bob Fink and Ron Turner at guards and Clark Taylor and Dwight Tallman at tackles helped clear the way for the dangerous DePauw backfield. "They were just blocking beautifully. They were doing a great job," Bryant said. "Tom Campbell, who was the other halfback who gained more yards than I did in that game, was a hell of a back."

All momentum was returned to Wabash by halftime when DePauw ceded its lead late in the second quarter. A touchdown pass from Little Giant quarterback Vic Lodovisi to Dennis Burdock with three minutes and forty seconds left in the half cut the lead to six. Two minutes later, Wabash end Tom Hankinson blocked a DePauw punt and Bill Gabbert recovered the ball at the DePauw fourteen-yard line. Lodovisi cashed in on the turnover on the second play when he couldn't find an open receiver and scrambled to his right all the way into the end zone. A missed extra point left the game tied at thirteen entering halftime.

The thirteen-point second quarter sparked a fire in Wabash that poured into halftime. A recorded speech by head coach Garland Frazier, who was in the hospital for an appendectomy, was played for the team as inspiration during the break. "Frazier was very emotional about it, and so was the team," Gabbert said. "He was a very stern, tough, Marine Corps–type guy, but in this speech, he actually broke down. You could tell his chin was quivering. It was quite emotional."

The Wabash momentum carried into the start of the third quarter, and a fourth-down gamble turned into six points. On fourth-and-eight at the DePauw nine-yard line, Lodovisi dropped back and floated a pass to Hankinson, who caught the ball at the goal line for a touchdown and the lead. A Little Giant extra point pushed the score to 20–13 in Wabash's favor.

A Lodovisi miscue later in the quarter allowed DePauw to put itself back in the game. DePauw end Jack Johnson recovered a Lodovisi fumble at the Wabash thirty-six-yard line. Seven plays later, Bryant scored once again, this time from two yards out, and a Williams extra point tied the game at twenty.

A back-and-forth final quarter appeared to have the game destined for the sixth tie in the history of the rivalry. Limited substitutions left tired players on the field trying to find one last gasp to pull out a win. DePauw took its chance on a fourth-and-two on its own forty-four-yard line. The offense lined up in a punt formation but relied on quarterback Morrie Goodnight's arm for a fourth-down conversion. Goodnight caught the long snap from the punter position, put his head down while taking two steps like a punter and pulled up to throw a pass to Dick Hackenberg in the left flat. Hackenberg caught the pass and turned up field into Wabash territory for the first down. Moments later, a pass from Goodnight over the middle of the field to end Gene Halladay put the Tigers at the ten-yard line. As the game entered its final minute, a one-yard gain by Bryant set up a second-and-goal. The clock continued to tick away as Goodnight looked to throw again. Knocked down by a defender, his incomplete pass left two seconds on the clock. Skip Mathieson looked over to the circular clock, which appeared to have no time left. "The hand was on the zero, but it hadn't tripped the buzzer to go off. I guess it had to get there first and then trip the buzzer," Mathieson said. "There was basically no time on the clock on that thing. It was obviously the last play of the game."

Fullback Skip Mathieson helped DePauw snap a six-year Monon Bell Classic losing streak in 1955 with a 23–20 win. *Courtesy of DePauw Archives.*

FIELD GOALS HADN'T served much of a purpose for DePauw in the four years Fred Williams was in the program. In addition to his fullback responsibilities, Williams took on the role of extra-point kicker. The brute force of his right leg usually provided enough distance and accuracy to drive the football between the goalposts off the front of his foot. "I did extra points, but in the previous four years I played, we never had an opportunity where a field goal would have done any good," Williams said.

That didn't stop Williams from fooling around a bit after practice with some kicks slightly longer than extra points. He thought he could make a field goal from as far out as twenty-five yards from his limited practice. So when Williams realized a last-second field goal was a possibility, he approached head coach Mike Snavely. "I looked up at him and I said, 'Hey, coach, I can do it. I can make it,'" Williams said. "I guess he said we're going to try it, so he sent me out there.

The level of confidence in Williams's ability to make the field goal measured out to roughly the same level of energy left in players like Jerry Rose and Art Bryant, who played all sixty minutes of the ball game. Rose had to gather himself to snap the ball. "I was pretty much out of it by the end. I can remember it," Rose said. "I can visualize being on the field. I can remember getting ready for the field goal. I was feeling good about the game but sort of being a little out of touch because [I was] so tired. I wasn't thinking too clearly."

Bryant felt the same exhaustion. "I was so damn tired I was just happy it was close to getting over," Bryant said. "Of course we were all hoping. I was

DePauw's Fred Williams, hero of the 1955 Monon Bell Classic, poses with the Bell. Williams kicked a last-second field goal, the first of his career, to lift the Tigers to a 23–20 win over Wabash. *Courtesy of DePauw Archives.*

blocking on one end of the line, and I got down in my stance and the Wabash guy didn't even charge. He just stood up and looked. So it was easy for me."

Rose snapped the ball back to holder Morrie Goodnight, who placed the ball down and let Williams give it a rip. Williams swung through with his right leg, and the pigskin tumbled end over end through the uprights. DePauw won 23–20 and earned the rights to the Monon Bell for the first time since 1948.

DePauw celebrated in amazement while Wabash players crumpled in astonishment. "In those days, a tie was a tie. There was no playoff," said Wabash's Bill Gabbert. "We all just presumed that this was going to be a tie game, and when it wasn't, it was pretty devastating."

Fred Williams couldn't wipe the smile off his face. The reserve fullback won a Monon Bell Classic with his right foot. "My one and only field goal in my four-year career," Williams said, "and it luckily snuck through the bars."

TO THIS DAY, Art Bryant has refused to remember the story differently. Nearly sixty years since the game happened, he could say he had all the confidence in the world that Fred Williams was going to make that kick. But when Bryant was asked if he thought that was the case fifty-eight years later, he remained honest. "Hell no," he said. "In fact, I don't think anybody thought he would make it. It was gorgeous. He put it right down the middle. He became 'Fred the Toe.' It made him famous, and it should have. It was tremendous."

Years of reflection have shown Jerry Rose that he probably should have been more nervous than he was in the moment. The thought of messing up the snap to holder Morrie Goodnight never crossed his mind, even if he had barely practiced the routine. "I never realized it until it was all over," Rose said. "I never feared it like, 'Oh my God. You could have really screwed that up.' But I never had a second thought, and I don't think he did either. It was just part of the game. 'Come on, we've got a chance. We've got a chance to beat them.' That's what we were thinking."

Williams's legend grew larger with his fellow students because his kick forced the hand of DePauw president Russell Humbert to follow through on a DePauw tradition. A Monon Bell victory bought the students an extra day off from classes. As a result, classes resumed the Tuesday after Thanksgiving Break rather than Monday.

The victory has wiped away Bryant's memories of the three losses suffered at the hands of Wabash during his time at DePauw. The last game of his college career has replaced those. "The campus went wild," Bryant said. "It was just one of those great days that you can't duplicate."

Except when a few members of the '55 team were all on campus at the same time fifty-some years later. Among others, Rose and Williams set out to

Blackstock Stadium for an impromptu reenactment of the kick. This time, Williams was slightly less prepared, but the result was the same. "All I had was a pair of tennis shoes and my running shorts," Williams said. "Luckily I squeaked it through."

Chapter 3

1962: A LITTLE MENIGHAN MAGIC

DEPAUW 13, WABASH 10

In the search for leaders of its football program, DePauw University didn't sell itself short in the spring of 1959. DePauw turned to Tommy Mont to take the reins of its small college football program. Mont came to DePauw with plenty of big-time football experience. After playing collegiately at the University of Maryland, Mont spent three years in the National Football League working as a defensive back and backup quarterback for the Washington Redskins, spending time behind future Hall of Famer Sammy Baugh.

Three years into a coaching career, Mont returned to Maryland to be an assistant coach under Jim Tatum. With Mont on staff, the Terrapins finished the 1951 season with a 10–0 record and the number-three ranking in the country in the final Associated Press poll. In 1953, a 10–1 Maryland team was named national champions by the AP. Mont took over the program in 1956 when Tatum left for North Carolina, but the former assistant coach couldn't find the same success as head coach. In three seasons, Mont's Maryland teams tallied a mediocre record of 11–18–1. That's when he decided to try his hand at DePauw.

Months into his new job in Greencastle, Mont brought in Ted Katula, who was also named as the head baseball coach, to be his assistant coach. Katula played collegiately at Ohio State University and came to DePauw following a stint as an assistant coach with Oberlin College. Mont became the offensive mastermind, and Katula took on defensive assignments. Together the two worked to turn around a football team in search of consistency, but the process took time. The first season, '59, ended with a 1–7–1 record. The following season found a two-game improvement for a 3–5–1 record. Then, in 1961, the Tigers finished 5–4 for their first winning season since 1957.

Success for DePauw in the Monon Bell Classic didn't disappear. The Tigers failed to lose a game to Wabash since 1954 despite two coaching changes. Mont's teams required dramatics to escape without a loss in his first two Monon Bell matchups. The '59 game ended in a 6–6 tie after the Tigers knotted the score in the third quarter and held Wabash from scoring from the two-yard line with ten seconds left in the game. In '60, John Rubush converted a two-point attempt with forty-eight seconds left in the game to give the Tigers a 14–13 victory. With his best team yet at DePauw, Mont's squad won the '61 game by a score of 20–7 in an easy home triumph.

Kit Lortz started the first game of his varsity career at DePauw under Mont. Lortz, the eldest son of George Lortz, a captain of the undefeated, untied and unscored-upon 1933 Tiger team that won the Monon Bell for the first time, played end as a sophomore in '59 and tackle in his junior and senior seasons. Following his playing career, Kit Lortz joined Mont's staff in 1962 as a graduate assistant while pursing a master's degree in mathematics. During the week, Lortz coached the linemen, and on Saturdays he traveled to scout future opponents. Lortz appreciated Mont as a coach but was leery about working on his staff. Mont didn't present a personable relationship with many of his players. "He was kind of an aloof person. In the good guy/bad guy thing, he was the bad guy. Katula was the good guy. They played that role on the football field," Lortz said. "Mont was a very complicated sort of person. He was very intelligent. He'd been in the big time for a while with Maryland and then with the Redskins. He was kind of a mystery to everybody. I knew Katula real well—as close as a coach and a player can be. Getting along with him was fine, but I was concerned about this deal with Mont. It couldn't have worked out better. Mont turned out to be a very different person off the field than on it. We became pretty good friends."

With an already impressive resume as a player and coach, Mont was popular for making speaking appearances across the state of Indiana. The head coach asked Lortz to tag along a few times, and that's when he began to understand the man behind the genius strategist. "He would make up these offenses and defenses and introduce them to the coaching staff and then to the team," Lortz said. "The whole week was pretty much putting in these new offenses and defenses for each particular team we were going to play. It was very interesting."

DePauw head coach Tommy Mont led his team to a victory in the 1962 Monon Bell Classic after making his team switch jerseys at halftime and letting quarterback Jim Menighan throw the ball more than usual. Here Mont crouches in front of his players during a game in 1963. *Courtesy of DePauw Archives.*

The '62 squad, much like his previous teams at DePauw and Maryland, featured a persistent running game. The brunt of the work fell on the shoulders of halfback Doug Weir and fullback Duff Gula, with quarterback Jim Menighan's role coming mostly with handoffs.

"Coach Mont was very innovative, but the innovation mostly came through running. He was a running coach," Lortz said. "To be quite honest with you, we never had any truly outstanding quarterbacks either. You take what you can get. That's where Mont was such a genius. He was able to take whatever talent he did have and build offenses and defenses around the personnel rather than trying to fit the personnel into something it really couldn't do."

As a result, DePauw entered the '62 Monon Bell Classic with a 4–4 record. A victory against Wabash would mark the second straight winning season for the Tigers and keep the Bell in Greencastle for an eighth straight year. The game would be Menighan's last at DePauw, and the senior would play an unexpected role.

"We didn't have the greatest athletes in the world on our teams, but we always had winning seasons," Menighan said. "Coach Mont got about as much out of the players as he possibly could."

Phil Eskew might not have ended up at DePauw if it wasn't for his mother. As a senior at Sullivan High School, Eskew took a close look at Wabash. He traveled to Crawfordsville one weekend to find out what kind of scholarships he could qualify for at the school. While taking a test on campus, Wabash head coach Garland Frazier pulled him out of the classroom and said he could offer Eskew a full scholarship based on his academics if he would come play football for him. Eskew had already been nudged toward Wabash by his high school government teacher, a Wabash graduate. A tuition-free education sounded awfully nice.

"My mother said, 'Nope. You are going to a school where you are going to learn manners, you're going to have a housemother, and you're going to experience the co-ed environment. You are not going to an all-boys school,'" Eskew said. "So I took a $50-per-semester scholarship and went to DePauw."

Eskew had a connection to the DePauw football program, too. Sullivan graduate Tom Campbell excelled as a halfback for the Tigers for two seasons following a highly touted career in high school. Campbell graduated in the spring of '59, just months before Eskew arrived on campus in the fall. "Tom was one of my idols growing up," Eskew said. "He was four years older, but he was a state champion in scoring and was just a great athlete. He tore his knee up, and that ended his career at DePauw, but he was also a great hurdler. I ran the hurdles as well, so I kinda followed Tom."

Sam Chattin had grander plans than college in Greencastle, too. He received a number of letters from bigger universities after his high school career at Lincoln High in Vincennes, Indiana. One particular letter from a certain school caught his eye: Florida State University. Chattin decided he would head down to Tallahassee in the fall of '59 to play football for the Seminoles.

However, Chattin hadn't broken the news of his decision to his father. Three days before he was set to head down to Florida, Chattin shared his plans with his father. It was greeted with silence. "I knew at that point that I probably wasn't going to join the Seminoles," Chattin said. The next morning, Chattin's father asked if he needed to do anything before he left, but Chattin had already packed a trunk for his travels. His father insisted on driving, so the two hopped in the car together the next morning. "He hadn't even read the letter or seen any of that yet," Chattin said. "As it wound up, he was not going to let me go there. He didn't care where it was as long as it had a good medical school." Chattin wasn't paying attention to the road, but his father started toward Greencastle, and before Chattin knew it, he was at DePauw.

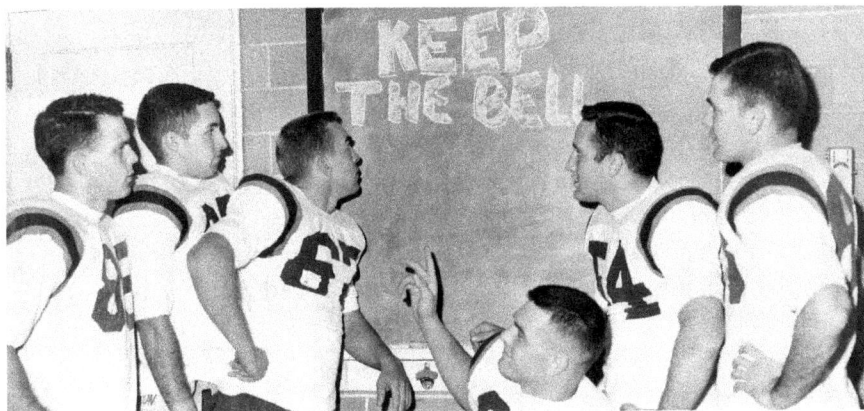

DePauw players gather for motivation before the 1962 Monon Bell Classic. The Tigers won the game by a 13–10 score. *Courtesy of DePauw Archives.*

"I arrived in good ole Greencastle, and we walked right to Coach Mont's office—Dad had already phoned him," Chattin said. "And within two hours, I was on the field in full dress with about another sixty to seventy freshman who I knew none of. Not one single guy did I know. That's how I arrived at DePauw."

In the coming months and years, Chattin learned to appreciate the decision his dad had made for him. He didn't try to fight it. "I loved my father beyond all things at the time, but he was a set man," Chattin recalled. "That was the way it was going to be, and there was no use even thinking about it. And I'm glad. To tell you the truth, I didn't know a whole lot about Florida State. In those days, it was the party school of the nation. I would have never become a doctor there. Of course, I didn't become a doctor anyway."

The realization that he wasn't better than the competition surrounding him at DePauw hit Chattin even quicker. "These guys were a whole lot better than I ever thought College Division football would be. I thought I was going to be like Superman or something like that. That's not the way it worked," Chattin said. "We had great guys. I know when Coach Mont got there and got his staff, they started bringing kids in from all over the United States."

INTENSITY AND PASSION for the rivalry remained through DePauw's long unbeaten streak over Wabash. The past seven years were filled with ties and close victories for the Tigers. DePauw assistant coach Ted Katula played a large role in firing up his squad each year for the Monon Bell Classic. "For some reason…we never figured out, Ted Katula hated Wabash. He would go berserk the week of Wabash preparation," said fellow assistant coach Kit Lortz. "Nobody could ever figure out what it was in Ted Katula that drove him nuts about Wabash. That was his game. He'd wait the whole season for that Wabash game, and then he would go absolutely bananas."

Not everyone at DePauw became as crazed in their dislike for Wabash as Katula. Senior end Sam Chattin said most hatred came from the student bodies, not the football teams. On the field, the play remained as clean as it can for a rivalry game. For Chattin, he found enjoyment in playing a team each year he respected even if he and his teammates were the butt of countless jokes in the Wabash student newspaper every November. "You can say anything you want to. It's what you do. That's all I looked at anything and anybody for—what you do," Chattin said. "Against us, they were literally Little Giants. That was a well-made title, Little Giants. How could you not fight with a title like that?"

The '62 Wabash team had plenty of fight in it. The Little Giants entered the sixty-ninth Monon Bell Classic with a 5–2–1 record on the season, their best resume prior to the DePauw game since 1956. In his second season as head coach, Ken Keuffel continued to employ a single-wing offense at Wabash. The offensive scheme slowly faded from college football, but Keuffel embraced the throwback style. The offense worked around the abilities of one singular talent at the tailback position who received the snap like a quarterback, engineered a dominant running offense, threw passes at times and even served as the team's punter.

Junior tailback Lynn Garrard fit the single-wing scheme perfectly, and when paired with Keuffel's play-calling and solid blocking on the line, the offense thrived. By the end of the '62 schedule, Garrard led the state in points scored with ninety-four. Garrard entered the home game against DePauw with eleven rushing touchdowns and eighteen extra points, threw for six passing touchdowns, and set a school record with a seventy-three-yard punt against Wheaton. Keuffel would need Garrard to deliver once again on a cold, muddy field to beat DePauw.

To start the game, Keuffel's single-wing offense hit the ground running. On the second play from scrimmage, fullback Allan Anderson took a handoff for fifty-four yards down to the DePauw sixteen-yard line. Tiger defensive back Phil Eskew, who made a point to stay clean during pregame warm-ups, found himself in the mud, thanks to a feeble attempt at tackling Anderson. "The fullback for Wabash came through the middle of the line, and I halfheartedly tried to tackle him and he went all the way down inside the twenty-yard line," Eskew said. "Of course at that point, I was wet and muddy. That changed my entire game from that point on because now I was ready to play, but I really screwed up by not being ready on those first plays."

Garrard made sure the Tigers regretted the sluggish start when he scored on a one-yard touchdown run moments later. He added the extra point, and the Bell-thirsty Little Giants jumped out to a 7–0 lead with ten minutes and fifty seconds left in the first quarter. DePauw's first drive reached the Wabash thirty-one-yard line, but the Tigers turned the ball over on fourth down.

Anderson and Garrard combined to produce another Wabash score late in the second quarter. DePauw quarterback Jim Menighan was given a rare green light to throw a few passes in the final minute, but one landed in the hands of Anderson in the Wabash secondary. Anderson returned the interception back to DePauw's fourteen-yard line with nineteen seconds left in the half. After a run to the ten-yard line on first down, Garrard knocked in a twenty-seven-yard field goal to give Wabash a 10–0 lead at halftime.

DEPAUW HEAD COACH TOM MONT didn't like what he saw from his team in the first half. His squad, with their white pants and white jerseys covered in mud, gathered around him in the locker room looking for answers to flip the script in the second half. Mont's first solution: change the jerseys. Anticipating the poor weather conditions, Mont had the equipment manager pack the team's black jerseys to come along to Crawfordsville with them as well. He decided to put the extra laundry to use.

"At halftime, you couldn't read the numbers on our jerseys," said DePauw safety Phil Eskew. "Coach Mont said we're going to change jerseys. I don't know whether he thought doing things like that was going to give us power or anything like that. He just simply said, 'We're changing jerseys, and we're going to go back out there and win this game.'" The switching of jerseys became Mont's first second-half adjustment. The players went ahead and swapped out their soggy whites for dry blacks and prepared for the final thirty minutes. "We had never done that before," said end Sam Chattin. "I'm not even so sure it was really something that the rules said you couldn't do. Apparently it wasn't, though."

When both teams emerged for the second half, the Wabash sideline looked across the field, puzzled by the new-look Tigers. Somehow, Mont managed to cause a subtle shift in the momentum of the game without a single play.

"These things are funny. I do remember that it was a psychological advantage—and who would know why that would be the case?" said Wabash fullback Allan Anderson. "It was muddy, and we were wet down to our bones. So here they come prancing out in the second half in clean jerseys."

Mont also decided to make a schematic change in the second half. After talking with assistant Ted Katula, the two decided to give quarterback Jim Menighan the chance to throw the ball more than he had all season. "Our coach was a control coach," Menighan said. "He would never let me call my own plays. He would never let me call audibles. It was the play that he called or no play at all. So we ran a lot. For four years, I was a frustrated passing quarterback." In Menighan's final Monon Bell game, Mont decided to give his quarterback one last shot. "He said, 'You got a half left in your career, go ahead and see what you can do.'"

Eskew, who practiced as a backup quarterback in addition to his role as a safety, knew Menighan had the arm to throw the ball around the field. He just hadn't seen Menighan live up to that potential in Mont's offense. Menighan's teammates and opponents alike hadn't witnessed a threatening DePauw passing attack.

"Needless to say, Wabash had no idea. They weren't expecting that at all. Who knew?" said DePauw assistant coach Kit Lortz. "Basically, our quarterbacks were option quarterbacks moving down the line, handing off or pitching out for sweeps or, on rare occasions, running a naked reverse. We just didn't practice throwing that much. We probably had maybe ten passing plays and probably two hundred running plays. We didn't run formations that were particularly suitable for passing, either. Mont was a running coach. He thought the name of the game was win it by running, and if you're not winning, try to pass to get back in the ball game."

Menighan did just that early in the second half. After the DePauw defense forced a Wabash punt, Menighan and the Tiger

End Sam Chattin caught the first of two touchdown passes from quarterback Jim Menighan in the second half of a 13–10 comeback victory for DePauw in the 1962 Monon Bell Classic. *Courtesy of DePauw Archives.*

offense started a drive at their own twelve-yard line. On the seventh play of the drive, Menighan floated a pass to Sam Chattin, who outleaped a Wabash defender at the goal line to haul in the touchdown reception. Menighan completed six straight passes on the drive to lead the Tigers into the end zone and cut the deficit to 10–6 with five minutes and seven seconds left in the third quarter. "I called a lot of hook passes and eight or ten yard outs. Because it was muddy and rainy, the guys knew where they were going, but the defenders had to play a little loose," Menighan said. "I'd see a guy out there at ten yards and throw it to him, twelve yards and throw it to him, fifteen yards and throw it to him. I couldn't throw deep in such bad weather because the football was wet, and I had little hands, so I couldn't grip it real well to let it rip. I don't know if I threw any balls over fifteen to twenty yards in that whole second half."

The aerial momentum carried over into DePauw's next drive. Menighan marched the team into Wabash territory after starting at the Tiger twenty-five-yard line. On fourth down, Menighan found Eric Christman in the end zone for a thirteen-yard touchdown completion. Richard Dean knocked through an extra point to push the Tigers to a 13–10 lead in the fourth quarter.

The Tiger defense was left to try to shut down the Wabash offense one more time and came through. The final threat from the Little Giants was ended when DePauw's John Thomas batted down a Lynn Garrard pass to give the ball back to Menighan and the offense to run the clock out on a 13–10 win.

Eskew and the rest of the DePauw defense kept the Little Giants grounded to complete the comeback. The Wabash offense managed to complete just one pass out of eleven attempts from their single-wing offense with Garrard at the helm from the tailback position. The Tigers surrendered only 184 yards of total offense to Wabash. "We had them on the ropes. Lynn Garrard was trying to throw these passes, and he just couldn't pass," Eskew said. "It was obvious that the only way they were going to score on us was running it, and our defensive linemen were doing well. He was throwing floaters that my other defensive backs and I were just not knocking down. The receivers had no chance to outrun us because he just couldn't throw the ball that far."

Menighan had much better luck. The senior quarterback finished the game completing fourteen of his twenty pass attempts for 186 yards and both DePauw touchdowns. He spread his passes to six different receivers, with Christman (four catches, 66 yards) and Ed Skeeters (four catches, 45 yards) leading the way. Menighan also led the Tigers in rushing yards with 47. With his confidence at an all-time high, he jabbed head coach Tom

Mont one last time. "It was one of the games where it's like a once-in-a-million type of thing," Menighan said. "So we wound up winning the game, and afterward the coach came up and said, 'Hey Jim, nice game.' I said, 'It could have been four seasons worth of that if you had let me throw the ball.' That was it. It was one of those wonderful endings to a career that didn't include a lot of passing."

Eskew and a few other mud-stained Tigers lifted Mont on their shoulders, carried him off the field and began a celebration with the Monon Bell for the eighth straight year.

Chapter 4

1967: THE MUD BOWL UPSET

WABASH 7, DEPAUW 0

A coaching change left the 1967 Wabash College football team in a tough spot. Gone was Ken Keuffel, champion of the single-wing offense. In came Max Urick, an assistant coach at Ohio State, and an overhaul of the entire offense. The first problem: the Wabash roster didn't include a true quarterback. Dave Knott, a returning junior, joined the program as a single-wing tailback, the same position he played at Valparaiso High School. The connection to Keuffel's scheme attracted Knott to Wabash, but now he'd have to learn a new position on the fly in order to make something of the final two years of his college career. Urick brought a modern offense and a different atmosphere to the Little Giants football team.

"It was kind of a culture shock," Knott said. "Ken Keuffel's background was in the Ivy League, and he actually taught a course in English literature. He was truly an academician. He was a good football coach, but he was also real faculty. Max Urick was a good football coach, too, but he thought football first and last. He wasn't an academician; he was a football coach. It was a different environment."

Urick had plenty of teaching to do on the field. Knott would need to transform into a traditional quarterback in a matter of months. The starting job was his to have for the season opener against Valparaiso University in his hometown. "The throwing the ball and handling the ball was easy because that's what single-wing tailbacks do," Knott said. "The hard part for me was the footwork, but I worked on it in the spring. We didn't have spring practice per se, but we worked out individually. By the time the season rolled around in September, I felt pretty comfortable. It really didn't take all that long. The mechanics of throwing the ball are the same. The footwork being under center and getting away from the center was a little bit different, but I got used to it pretty quickly."

The execution of the transition wasn't pretty. The Wabash offense struggled all season long. After the first win of the season, a 22–21 victory over Earlham College in week three, the Little Giants lost five games in a row heading into the season finale against DePauw. Wabash scored just 51 points in eight games for a 1–7 record and was held scoreless in four of the seven losses. "We were struggling. I'm in my first year as a head coach. I'm in over my head," Urick said. "We had just taken over and put a new offense in. I followed a great coach who had run the single wing at Wabash very successfully for years, Ken Keuffel. I didn't know much about the single wing, so we changed to a more conventional offense, and trying to make that transition had a set of challenges like none I had ever seen before. I wasn't very adept at making that kind of a transition. I was a terrible head coach that year. I was really on a learning curve."

Still, the Wabash players showed patience with their new head coach. They came out to practice every day and busted their tails while Urick tried to piece together a team worthy of its players' hard work. "They were just so devoted and had so much pride in being an all-men's school. They would just never give up," Urick said. "They'd go out to practice even though we were having a tough year and had disappointments along the way. They really would just fight to the end. And they were so tolerant of me being a 'green' coach that I always felt greatly indebted to them. They were terrific young men."

And as is always the case in Crawfordsville, a season-ending triumph over DePauw could redeem a lost season.

MEANWHILE, THE 1967 SEASON provided much better results for the Tigers of DePauw. Carrying over the momentum from a 9–7 Monon Bell victory over Wabash to end the 1966 season, the Old Gold squad put together its best campaign to date under head coach Tom Mont. A tie with Evansville and loss to Ball State stood as the only blemishes in a six-win season.

A potent offensive attack highlighted the successful DePauw team. Scoring 143 points and routinely tallying more than three hundred yards per game, the offense was led by a pair of quarterbacks—Dan Breckenridge and Eric Lortz—and a backfield trio of John Butler, John Sacramento and Bill Holton. Mont, starting to use the passing game more and more, rotated the two quarterbacks depending on the situation. Breckenridge possessed the better arm, and Lortz's strength came in running the ball. "Dan was a much better passer than I was. I was the running quarterback," Lortz said. "The good news for me was that Mont was a running-game coach. It wasn't like I couldn't throw. I threw a lot of passes. When we were behind in a game, Dan would come in. He was a good athlete, a good thrower, and he helped us out in that aspect."

Lortz, the youngest son of George Lortz, a captain of the undefeated, untied and unscored upon 1933 DePauw team that won the Monon Bell for the first time, had a winning tradition to uphold. He became the first Lortz son to lose a game to Wabash when the Tigers dropped their first game against the Little Giants in ten years in 1965. Older brothers Kit and Jeff avoided any losses during their four years in Greencastle in the middle of the unbeaten streak.

Eric Lortz desperately needed to end his DePauw career with another Monon Bell victory to avoid playful scorn at family gatherings. But the Tigers didn't have the assistance of '66 Monon Bell hero Tim Feemster, who knocked in the game-winning field goal in the seventy-third Monon Bell Classic, as a leg injury prevented him from playing his senior season and forced his legacy to end on a high-note.

DePauw assistant coach Ed Meyer knew the satisfaction that came with winning the Monon Bell game as a senior. He won his second Monon Bell game in his final year as a player in 1961. Now a coach, the importance of winning the game meant job security. "Coach Mont would tell you in those days that no matter how you did during the season, if you beat Wabash, you always had a job," Meyer said. "It was the most important game on our schedule. We spent a lot of time worrying about them."

A win over Wabash would keep DePauw's hopes alive for a postseason trip to one of the four bowl games in the NCAA College Division. Wabash, with a little help from the weather, had other plans.

DAVE HUSTED DIDN'T HAVE any problem understanding the rivalry between the Tigers and Little Giants. By the time he became a junior at Wabash in 1967, his list of reasons to dislike the foes in Greencastle grew from stereotypical to personal. "It was just sort of a given that everybody there disliked DePauw. It was one of those things that was sort of drilled into everybody from the beginning," Husted said. "The Dannies were pictured as a little arrogant, carrying umbrellas wherever they went and also having all the girlfriends. That was a problem, too."

When Husted graduated from Thomas Carr Howe High School in Indianapolis in 1965, he left a younger girlfriend, Laurie Detamore, back at home. The two stayed together for most of his first two years at Wabash, but in 1967, she graduated and headed to DePauw to join her older brother Trent, who played football for the Tigers. Husted and Detamore's relationship took a hit. "A lot of the guys from Wabash had gone to school with people from DePauw, and so we were constantly getting fixed up with girls down there that people knew," Husted said. "We either went there or Purdue or IU for dates, and that was pretty much the extent of it. There were definitely hard feelings. Wabash was a fairly demanding school scholastically, so we had to study a lot. People blew off steam and vented a lot of that steam at DePauw."

Husted thought Detamore attending DePauw would be a positive with her being only a half-hour drive away. Then it became clear to Husted that she didn't want him around anymore. When Husted heard word that Detamore was hanging out with a DePauw football player, his animosity for the annual gridiron rivalry only grew more intense. "I remember just being angry throughout the whole game. I think all of us were," Husted said. "Everybody took it pretty personally."

Husted's frustration would be short-lived. He and Detamore ended up back together in the winter, and the two later married. But for the time being, Husted had another reason to push himself against DePauw.

THE BAD WEATHER started in the middle of the week leading up to the Monon Bell matchup. A cold November in central Indiana brought a mix of rain and snow in the days leading up to the DePauw-Wabash game at Blackstock Stadium. The Greencastle ground froze over on Friday night, but by the time both teams took the field on Saturday, the cold ground starting melting and producing copious amounts of mud.

Sloppy conditions favored the visiting Little Giants team. Both teams would be limited offensively, but Wabash would have a better chance of battling out a win in an ugly fashion. The weather figuratively leveled and literally softened the playing field. A game of slop potato ensued.

"You couldn't read the lines," said Wabash quarterback Dave Knott. "You could hardly tell the light shirts from the dark shirts. You couldn't even tell who was on whose team. Everybody was just covered in mud. It was covering your shoes. It was up to your ankles, and there was standing water. The whole game just became a war of attrition. Who can hold on to the ball and run three plays without fumbling?"

Not much white was left to be seen on the Wabash uniforms in the 1967 Monon Bell Classic, known as the Mud Bowl. The Little Giants were still able to pull off a 7–0 upset over the home team DePauw. *Courtesy of DePauw Archives.*

Ball security proved to be a problem for DePauw in the muddy conditions. More drives ended in turnovers (seven) than punts (six) throughout the game for the Tigers. Both teams ended the first half without a score, but a draw was a moral victory for Wabash. The Little Giants weren't supposed to be keeping pace with the home Old Gold squad.

"Our locker room…was jumping like it was just before the kickoff," Wabash head coach Max Urick said of the halftime atmosphere. "You couldn't talk. Everybody was jumping around. They couldn't wait to get back on the field again. I just looked around at the coaches kinda wide-eyed. I had never seen anything like this before. Our guys were loose. They said they felt like they could win."

The Wabash offense continued to pound the ball on the ground with short-yardage plays. Tailback Wayne Monroe and fullback Mike Henry carried the brunt of the work from the backfield following behind linemen like captain Randy Slickers at center.

"There were only about three or four of us that ever handled the ball," Knott said. "We were actually able to move the ball. As the game went on, we started thinking we could win simply because we seemed to be playing relatively normal football while they seemed to be reacting to the rain more than we were."

Wayne Monroe trudged his way into the DePauw defense carry after carry with the yardage slowly adding up. He finished the game with forty-four rushing attempts for 143 yards. "I carried the ball a lot of times, but for just 4, 5 and 6 yards and kept grinding them out. We were keeping DePauw on defense," Monroe said. "With the weather conditions, that was about the only thing you could do. The passing game was pretty rough that day with the weather such as it was. The linemen did a good job of rooting them out, opening a little hole and giving me a little daylight."

The biggest carry of the game came from Henry, whose two-yard plunge capped the first Wabash drive of the second half and gave the Little Giants their first touchdown of the game. Kicker Terry Schuck added the extra point to give Wabash a 7–0 lead early in the third quarter. A Wabash upset soon became a distinct possibility, if not a predictable eventuality, after forty-five minutes of game play. "That touchdown was just a couple yards, but it was a tough couple yards," Henry said. "I played only in short-yardage situations my sophomore year, so they pretty much knew who was getting the ball. But it was a mess."

Defensive end Dave Husted and the rest of the Wabash defenders held DePauw in check for the remainder of the game. "Because of the weather, that enabled us to hang in there," Husted said. "It slowed the DePauw offense down so much. … We had pretty big, strong guys. We were able to control the line on defense particularly." The Tigers used forty-two carries to net a measly seventy-four yards rushing. Similarly stymied, the passing attack, featuring quarterbacks Dan Breckenridge and Eric Lortz, completed only seven of twenty-five passes for ninety yards and four interceptions. Three DePauw fumbles added to the misery.

The underdog Little Giants emerged victorious. The mud-stained white Wabash uniforms practically matched the darkness of the black DePauw jerseys. The two worthy foes looked more alike than rivals should at the end of the game. "I think we actually were the better team that day," Knott said. "If you talk to a DePauw guy, they probably wouldn't remember it that way."

The memory hasn't left Eric Lortz, whose four-year football career at DePauw ended with a loss to Wabash. "What has lived with me throughout life, believe it or not, is that my last football game was a major disappointment,"

DePauw's Eric Lortz attempts a punt in the 1967 Monon Bell Classic, known as the Mud Bowl. Lortz, also a quarterback for the Tigers, was unable to lead the DePauw offense to a score the entire game. *Courtesy of DePauw Archives.*

Lortz said. "The weather was terrible. Our strength was throwing the ball. Of course we couldn't do that. They were small and fast, and we were big and strong, but that didn't help us on a day like that. They were just quicker and outhustled us, if you want to know the truth. It was a real big blow. I can only tell you that a loss of a Wabash game for a DePauw athlete lives with you for a long time, if not forever."

The fact that his legacy ended so much differently from his father and older brothers only added to the pain. George Lortz '34, Kit Lortz '62 and Jeff Lortz '65 all endured DePauw careers without a loss to Wabash. Eric Lortz left DePauw with a pair of Ls in his three years on the varsity team. "They've often let me know that over my lifetime," Eric Lortz said. "It never goes away."

What was hidden, though, was the Monon Bell. The three-hundred-pound ringer went missing from DePauw's campus that fall, with few admitting any idea where the bell was located. One rumor around Greencastle claimed Wabash swiped the Bell and had it stowed away in a Crawfordsville bank.

After a handful of students pulled off a legendary heist of the Bell under the guise of a visiting Mexican reporter in 1965, DePauw students had plenty of reasons for paranoia.

The DePauw choir hoped to use the Bell the Friday night before the game, but it hadn't surfaced. The game ended on Saturday with still no sign of the Bell. That's when DePauw students started digging beyond the north end zone. Fearing another theft, some students buried the Bell, where it sat silent the entire game.

The Little Giants made plenty of noise of their own in the postgame celebration in the locker room. First-year head coach Max Urick joined in the jubilation, showering in his already filthy and soaked clothes. He would have plenty of time to ring the Bell on Wabash's campus in the next year.

Chapter 5

MONON BELL SHENANIGANS: TALES OF VANDALISM AND THEFT

C ountless entries litter the rivalry rap sheet for DePauw and Wabash. Vandalism and theft became part of the annual tradition early in the history between the two schools. Once the Monon Bell joined the fray, it birthed ingenuity in students looking to craft the perfect heist. But before the Bell became the center of attention, campus shenanigans played a large role.

Unwanted red paint made an appearance on DePauw's campus as early as 1924. A few Wabash students trekked to Greencastle the Thursday night before the annual clash. The visitors left their marks in scarlet on campus walkways and buildings before the Little Giants and their faithful fans arrived on Saturday. A similar act occurred again in 1930, when vandals returned to Blackstock Field the night before the game with plenty of red paint in tow. A prediction was painted across the back of the press box seats: "Wabash 32, DePauw 0." More red coated the both goals' posts, the scoreboard and the field entrance. The gate proclaimed, "Wabash Students Admitted Free." Admittance wouldn't be free, but the glares from the opposite side would be.

The stakes rose in 1941 when the Bell went missing from Wabash's campus in the fall. After months of worrying, including rumors that the Bell had been scrapped for its metal by the thieves, the trophy made an appearance in front of Jordan Hall on Butler University's campus a day before the Bulldogs were set to host DePauw. The Tigers lost to Butler in October and Wabash later in November, but the Bell was returned safely to one of the two campuses it calls home.

Monon Bell Represents Traditional Symbol Of Oldest Football Rivalry in Middle West

An editorial cartoon depicts the Monon Bell rivalry in 1948. *Courtesy of DePauw Archives.*

At least eight more Monon Bell heists have been reported in the campus newspapers for Wabash, *The Bachelor*, and DePauw, *The DePauw*. What follows are tales related to each memorable act of mischief.

1953: Two hundred Wabash students made their way to DePauw's campus in late September to find their missing Monon Bell. Met by a number of DePauw students and Greencastle Police, the Wabash mob spent most of its time shouting "We want the Bell!" and "Blood! Blood!" Accepting that a resolution wasn't coming that night, the Wabash students headed back home in short order.

Days later, a group of DePauw students returned the Bell to Crawfordsville. David W. Robinson, assistant dean of students, traveled with the group to meet Wabash dean Byron Trippet. The Bell was delivered to its storage space in the Wabash gymnasium. A handful of Little Giants made their way to confront the DePauw visitors, but they left safely without further conflict.

1959: Wabash took its turn at stealing the Bell in the fall of '59. The Little Giants failed to defeat DePauw for four years in a row on the gridiron, so the rivalry reached further into the student body. In order to guarantee a personal encounter with the Bell, a handful of Wabash students concocted a plan to locate the trophy using the fabricated identity of a high school newspaper reporter. Forced to return the Bell after a successful heist, the masterminds wrote an anonymous letter for *The Bachelor* explaining the executed plan. The letter, titled "To Borrow a Bell," appeared as such:

> When one is interested in borrowing a Monon Bell, there are certain steps he should take. First, one should find an effeminate, emasculate, rival institution, which has possession of such a bell. Then find a sly and poised Wabash student and christen him "Harry Highschool." One should outfit him with a senior class key, a National Honor Society pin, and a Crawfordsville license plate.
>
> This young man may then descend upon that poor, innocent, defenseless lace-pantied school to get some information. Oh, yes, he's a reporter on the high school paper, "The Black and Blue," and he would like to do a special story on the Monon Bell. Next semester, he might be made feature editor if the story is good enough. And he is interested in entering as a journalism student next fall. The director of admissions is very much interested in gaining what appears to be a full-male student, for once. He encourages the aspiring high schooler and sends him off to the director of athletics, who is the only person allowed to show the Monon Bell to anyone. The friendly admissions officer says, "Good luck in your quest," as the reporter goes out the door.

The director of athletics is busy, but this earnest face appeals to him. He calls up the student equipment manager, who rides over to the gym in a car which has only lately had a Wabash decal scraped off the back window. In due time, they reach the gym basement and a special view of the bell. "Yes, this is the bell. Pretty, isn't it?" And bidding adieu to the last of a line of gullible Dannies, our young spy heads back to C'Ville with his information.

It is not hard to plot the location of the basement room on the earlier prepared floor plan, and you are ready for a night of fun and profit. There's really no hurry, for Dannies never worry about the bell.

All is quiet, so you go over and lift up one of the gym windows. "There's no sense in locking the gym windows. We all like each other here at KittyKat Tech. No one would bother our happy togetherness." So you trot on through the locker room. There's the door. Handle your crowbar gently; don't chip any of that baby-pink paint off the door.

The door opens, and there is the Monon Bell, just where they showed it to you before. You pick it up and you're off. It's up the stairs, out the door, down the steps, and over to the street. The trailer gate is out, and the men on the outside report no business at all. In goes the bell, down goes the gate, and you set off for old Wabash. The night watchman says he was behind a tree, but then Dannies are always hiding.

Back at Wabash with the Monon Bell in true safekeeping, you settle down to your normal existence. But down at Dannyville, things are in a sorry state. "Someone tore the molding off the door where the swimming team's water wings are kept. They chipped the baby-pink paint. And they took the Monon Bell! What shall we do?" "I saw Broderick Crawford in 'State Trooper' on TV last night. He is big and strong and intelligent. Maybe he could do what we can't." So they called the State Police.

They called it "breaking and entering," and we had to take it back. But we expect the Monon Bell to stay in Dannyville no longer than November 14, when the Little Giant football team goes down to get it.

So the next time you get interested in borrowing a Monon Bell, make sure you pick a night when only the 'Mickey Mouse Club' is on TV.

1965: The longest drought in Monon Bell history inspired its greatest thievery. Wabash, failing to win against DePauw for ten straight years, was starving for time with the three-hundred-pound locomotive dinger. So in October 1965, a group of students started hatching a plan to lift the Bell from DePauw. By the end of the month, the plot was ready to take place.

In the 1960s, the Monon Bell started requiring more protection from thieves. Here the Bell sits in a truck bed on DePauw's campus. *Courtesy of DePauw Archives.*

Ringleader of the robbery, Jim Shanks, arranged a meeting with DePauw president William Kerstetter for Monday, November 1. Shanks used the guise of a Mexico City news reporter working on a college brochure for the United States Information Service. He also expressed an interest in connecting DePauw to Mexican students through the fictional Mexican-American Cultural Institute.

The lunch meeting, also attended by Louis Fontaine, director of admissions and financial aid, and Robert Farber, dean of the university, went as planned. During the discussion, Shanks expressed a keen interest in the Monon Bell and asked if he could take photos with the trophy. Kerstetter, not knowing where the Bell was being kept, asked his secretary, who responded with, "The last time I told a visitor where the Bell was, Wabash stole it."

Kerstetter dialed athletic director James Loveless, who met Shanks at an equipment building near Blackstock Stadium. Skeptical of Shanks's motives, Loveless asked to see his credentials. He failed to look close enough to realize

Left: Wabash student Jim Shanks famously stole the Monon Bell from DePauw in 1965 while posing as a Mexico City news reporter. He used his assumed identity to learn where the DePauw administration kept the Bell before returning with fellow classmates to steal the trophy. *Courtesy of DePauw Archives.*

Below: Wabash fans poked fun at DePauw by sporting sombreros and ponchos at the 1965 Monon Bell Classic. Weeks earlier, Wabash students had stolen the Bell from DePauw using the identity of a fake Mexican reporter to enable the heist. *Courtesy of DePauw Archives.*

that the press card wasn't accurate. Loveless led Shanks into the storage area and let him snap some photos of the Bell. Shanks left Greencastle, but no one on campus knew he was headed back to Wabash.

Later that evening, Shanks returned with a crew ready to break into the equipment room and take back the Bell. Another group, charged with creating a distraction for campus police, went to a female dorm to cause a ruckus. The disturbance bought Shanks and his buddies enough time to remove the Bell from the building and lift it into a car trunk headed back for Wabash.

A sight to be seen only on DePauw's campus: female students ringing the Monon Bell won by their male classmates. *Courtesy of DePauw Archives.*

The Bell would eventually be returned to DePauw before the '65 game, but the comical story spread on both campuses. Fully amused by Shanks's heist, some members of the Wabash student body wore ponchos and sombreros to the game. As an added bonus, the football team came through with a 16-6 victory and allowed the students to legally take the Bell back to Crawfordsville.

Looking to spin the blunder in his favor, Kerstetter told *The DePauw* that the events were "unique in my experience. No one else has ever faked it before with me. I guess it just illustrates the hospitality of DePauw."

1966: A DePauw win brought the Monon Bell back to Greencastle on Saturday, November 10, but the Tigers experienced trouble keeping track of it. Roughly a half hour after the Bell arrived back on DePauw's campus, a group of Wabash students regained possession of the trophy its football team had just lost. They followed the truck transporting the Bell and scooped it up when no one was watching. Wabash returned the Bell on Monday.

1973: Another DePauw heist sent a large mass of Wabash students to Greencastle to try and force their foes to return the Monon Bell. The Bell was being held inside the Sigma Alpha Epsilon fraternity house on campus. Fred Miller provided this personal recollection for the Wabash College Student News Bureau on October 16:

We got the Monon Bell back last night. We Wabash men did. It took about 200 of us with a little muscle, but we got it back from DePauw's SAEs.

The SAEs pulled off one of the slickest capers in the history of the Bell in stealing it from the gym lobby here Sunday night.

Getting the Bell back was of particular personal gratification to me since the president of the SAEs is a good friend. And so, this is my account of how we—my Wabash brothers and me—went to DePauw and brought the Bell back to its rightful home.

I got a phone call last night about 11 o'clock from a friend at the Phi Psi House. He told me to announce to members of my fraternity that about 75 or 100 Betas, Sigs, Delts and Phi Psis were leaving at midnight to go get the Bell from the DePauw SAEs. A DePauw sorority had tipped us off that the SAEs had taken it and were holding it in their house.

I made the announcement, and it seemed like the house emptied in seconds. That Bell means a lot to Wabash students.

We loaded up a car and went over to the Sigma Chi house and were told that many cars had just left. Fine. We took off in hot pursuit. About eight cars pulled into Greencastle with us, and a car "with two cherries on top" joined our caravan.

We cruised past the SAE house (the rest of the campus was either asleep, scared or studying), and we were hissed and chanted at. We parked our cars about three blocks away where we met other Wabash men.

A grisly, motley crew it was that started walking, chanting, anticipating a violent confrontation. As we walked, carloads of Cavemen pulled over, piled out and joined in the "march on the SAE house." There must have been 200 of us by now—some armed with clubs, other with bats and fire extinguishers.

We paraded into the front lawn of the SAE house and had a welcoming party of Greencastle's best and campus security. But this didn't stop us. We wanted that Bell. We sang "Old Wabash" and chanted "Give us the Bell"…and a few other nice things.

Peace didn't last long. Some of our guys had made their way to the back of the house and were attempting to scale the wall. The SAES, by this time, were building their forces in their basement and were guarding the safe that contained the Bell. This is no ordinary safe, however. It's 12 feet tall, four inches thick…steel on all four sides. I've seen it—I know. Also, only three Dannies know the combination. Wabash had a "demolition expert" on hand, but I don't think he would have done us much good.

Wabash now had control of the house—except for the basement. The SAE wasn't about to give it up without a big fight.

About that time, I thought I'd better try and talk to an opponent friend, Dean Wright. We went inside to discuss the whole thing. We surveyed the damage, and I knew that the Wabash men outside were bent on getting the Bell. The agreement: Dean Moore and Dean Wright would exchange the Bell at a neutral site before the annual football game.

Well, our Wabash crowd, growing all the while, didn't want it that way. They wanted it right then. Mike Eckerle, president of the Wabash IFC, came on the scene, and once again another meeting was held to try and work out something about the Bell.

It must be noted that the police had called out their "riot squad" and a few more Dannies were filtering in. It had the markings of a potential riot.

Wright, Eckerle and a few others talked it out and came to an agreement. In order to save the SAE house and DPU campus from destruction, SAE agreed to give the bell over to Eckerle in a neutral area. Only Eckerle and the SAE president would know the whereabouts of the Bell until game time.

Well, the crowd reluctantly agreed, sort of. We hadn't gotten the Bell, but the Dannies didn't have it either.

The situation is about back to normal here at Wabash, and we've been assured that we have the Bell.

1978: Another routine robbery, this time involving DePauw students extracting the Monon Bell from the Wabash gymnasium, incited more drama when students in Crawfordsville didn't take too kindly to their prized possession being stolen. Much like before, a mob of Little Giants trekked to Greencastle to demand their Bell back. Days earlier, Wabash officials insisted they would not step in and ask DePauw to return the Bell. According to *The Bachelor*, students were asked "to conduct themselves as gentlemen at all times in their efforts to retrieve the Bell." A Thursday night in late October unfolded quite differently.

An estimated three hundred Wabash men made their way to DePauw with baseball bats, bricks and broken bottles. The Little Giant protesters visited a sorority and various fraternity houses, making demands. In return,

Long removed from its old locomotive home, the Monon Bell requires transportation by the winning team to and from the annual rivalry game between DePauw and Wabash. *Courtesy of DePauw Archives.*

members of the DePauw student body gathered to protect their campus. The conflict remained mostly nonviolent but showed no signs of ending any time soon. Greencastle City Police, Indiana State Police and the Putnam County Sheriff's Department were all called onto campus to separate the mob. One DePauw woman and ten Wabash men were arrested for disorderly conduct before the quarrel died down.

Arrangements were made for the return of the Bell, but DePauw's administration felt the need to respond to what it called a "potential riot." President Richard Rosser met the next day with student senators and living-unit presidents to address campus safety. As a result, he issued a campus memo trying to create guidelines for future Monon Bell hijinks. His points:

- The Monon Bell competition is a great contest which is valued by both schools.

- Attempts to steal the Monon Bell are often a part of this competition, but in no case must attempts be made to recover the Bell on the other campus.
- The group stealing the Bell promises to return it to the campus from which it was stolen within 48 hours. If this is not done, the presidents of the two schools will seriously consider cancellation of the football game that year.
- Behavior during the game itself must reflect restraint on both sides, or else the game will be cancelled the following year—if not during the game itself.

Students on both campuses reacted unfavorably to the proposed rules, especially the threat of cancelling the annual game at the center of the storied rivalry. Wabash president Lewis Salter told *The DePauw* that he admired Rosser's idea to return the Bell within forty-eight hours but also realized its flaw. "There has always been a competing tradition where the people who manage to filch the Bell return it at the beginning of the game to applause the mob," Salter said.

DePauw students made a scene of their own upon returning the stolen item. The Monon Bell was ceremoniously returned to Wabash in a trade at Monument Circle in Indianapolis with alumni and media present. DePauw handed over the Bell in exchange for the bolt cutters the thieves left behind at the scene of the crime.

1978: Another successful heist by DePauw resulted in more trips for Wabash students to Greencastle. After small items were stolen from DePauw's campus on multiple occasions, Rosser reportedly threatened to step in to end the conflict. Much like the previous year, a warning of cancelling the game was presented and in turn greeted with disapproval. A group of Wabash students wrote a letter to the editor of *The DePauw* expressing their displeasure with the situation:

Dear Editor:

We are shocked (but not surprised) at the action of DePauw President Rosser in dealing with the theft of the Monon Bell from the Wabash campus Aug. 28. According to published reports, Rosser has threatened to have any Wabash students arrested if caught trying to get back the bell on the DePauw campus. This just isn't sporting! Theft of the bell is a tradition, and nobody at Wabash denies DePauw's right to attempt to steal it.

Wabash fans unfurl a banner in support of their team. *Courtesy of DePauw Archives.*

It's only fair that Rosser should reciprocate, especially as he invoked his double standard at a critical time.

A lot of Cavemen are hopping mad, not only that the bell was stolen, but that both this year and last the Rosser Youth that pilfered it have destroyed school property and possibly have damaged the bell itself. When Wabash students destroyed property at DePauw, Wabash students paid to have that property restored. Not so with Rosser. What more, he has threatened to cancel the annual game if Wabash men show up en masse at DPU.

Is he afraid of violence? We remember that last year, the Caveman hordes came down to Greendingle unarmed and that it was the Rosser Youth that was armed to the teeth with ropes, clubs, chains, baseball bats, and field hockey sticks. Maybe Rosser has ulterior motives for cancelling the game, namely DePauw's won-lost record.

The problem is simple. President Rosser doesn't think it's fair for 850 nasty, filthy, and crude Cavemen (just ask the Thetas) to pick on a school only two-and-one half times bigger. Well Pres, if you want to cancel the game, go ahead. You Dandies, keep the game. Let the men of Wabash keep the bell!

—*Eleven Men of Wabash College*

Above: A tiger poses with the Monon Bell. *Courtesy of DePauw Archives*.

Left: Tyler the Tiger and Wally Wabash fake a fight at the 2000 Monon Bell Classic. *Courtesy of DePauw Archives*.

The stolen items were later returned in exchange for the Bell in the small town of Parkersburg between Crawfordsville and Greencastle.

1988: A few Wabash students hid in DePauw's Lilly Center following a basketball loss to the Tigers. Left alone in the gymnasium at night, the Little Giants escaped with the Bell.

1998: Mimicking the efforts of Wabash students a decade prior, an overnight stay in the Lilly Center was used to steal the Monon Bell away from DePauw once again. When campus staff noticed the Bell was missing from its perch inside Neal Fieldhouse on the morning of Halloween, the first assumption was that it had been moved in preparation for an upcoming concert. When DePauw Police learned that athletic director Page Cotton and head coach Nick Mourouzis didn't know the whereabouts of the Bell, it became clear it had been stolen.

The thieves left little evidence, and the Lilly Center had no signs of a forced entry. The police were baffled until the story of the robbery was detailed on Wabash's campus in *The Bachelor* almost a week later. Pictures of the culprits wearing ski masks in the DePauw gymnasium provided further proof of their proud achievement.

Eight students took part in the heist with the help of a non-assuming DePauw student. Entrance to the Lilly Center required a swipe of a valid student ID, but the DePauw student let in the unknown Wabash conspirator without second judgment. Once inside, the Wabash student hid in the ceiling tiles above the men's bathroom for the night. After the building closed, he climbed down from the ceiling and opened the door for his seven friends.

From there, the Wabash group used scaffolding already in the gym to reach the Bell's perch high on the wall. After carefully lowering the Bell, the students used a wheeled volleyball cart to roll the trophy to the exit door with the least amount of noise and resistance. The Bell then began its trip back to Crawfordsville with its new borrowers.

MORE THAN THE MONON BELL was stolen in the fall of 1998. After DePauw waxed Wabash by a score of 42–7, rumors swirled about the DePauw coaching staff stealing the offensive play signals of the Wabash coaching staff. The rumor grew legs because DePauw volunteer assistant coach Herb King boasted about the feat at a local church gathering in Crawfordsville. His pride in a DePauw victory apparently trumped his worry about breaking one of the Ten Commandments.

Former DePauw player Tim Hreha was hired in 1978 as an assistant coach for DePauw. He enters his thirty-fifth season with the program in 2013. *Courtesy of DePauw Archives.*

By December, the story grew from a big fish tale into an ethical discussion. DePauw head coach Nick Mourouzis received a call from Wabash head coach Greg Carlson asking if what he heard was true: had DePauw scouted Wabash multiple times and stolen signals? Mourouzis confirmed the rumor. He had nothing to hide and felt his staff had done nothing wrong. A disagreement commenced. It didn't matter, as defensive coordinator Tim Hreha would later assert, if DePauw hadn't taken advantage of the stolen signals until after opening up a 35–0 lead in the first half. Even then, Hreha said, the few decoded signals King relayed came in situations when Hreha already had a strong indication of the play because of film study.

"I was really mad because I thought we were as well prepared defensively as I could have gotten us," Hreha said. "I'm saying, 'Hey, we did a great job preparing ourselves.' To have a guy tell us that the reason we stopped them was because we knew the signals…to have them throw that crap up…why do you have a different guy signal in signals? Why do the NFL guys and college coaches cover their mouths when they're giving signals?"

Mourouzis caught heat for his stance, particularly from one Wabash alumnus, who described the actions he heard secondhand as "embarrassing and shameful" in a letter he wrote to Mourouzis and DePauw administrators.

On January 6, 1999, Mourouzis received another letter—this one from the American Football Coaches Association (AFCA)—detailing ethical violations filed against him by Carlson. He was asked to speak in front of the AFCA Ethics Committee the next week for a ruling.

Armed with excerpts from the NCAA Manual for Division III, Mourouzis delivered a carefully crafted speech explaining why he felt his coaching staff had done no wrong. On the topic of improper scouting, he explained that since DePauw had left Wabash's conference for the Southern Collegiate Athletic Conference in 1998, it was not limited in the number of games it could scout Wabash. He argued that his staff had the right to fairly find a competitive advantage:

> In regard to "stealing," reading, or observing signals: college football, at all levels, is a very competitive sport. Coaching staffs and players spend countless hours preparing for games in an effort to provide their teams with the best possible opportunity to perform well on the field. As a coach or player, you should expect that the opposing team will pay attention to your actions and words. Your opponents do, and are expected to, pay attention to your players, your formations, your plays, the tendency to run certain plays from certain formations, the strengths and weaknesses of your team, and even newspaper quotations. On the field, players and coaches look and listen to what an opponent does or says, including audibles, signals, and any instructions yelled or otherwise relayed from coach to player or player to player. Because teams expect opposing teams to pay attention is why teams often take significant precautions to disguise and protect their communication.
>
> After Albion College "stole" or read our offensive signals six years ago, we began sending in our plays with wide receivers. I did not object to the actions of the Albion staff because I felt that their actions were part of the game. But I learned from the experience! Similarly, because Wabash knows our offense three-step drop-back series that we use as a check at the line of scrimmage, we have over the years adopted a different code system designed and specifically used for Wabash.
>
> Based on my many years of experience coaching NCAA football and my knowledge of college football's rules and norms of behavior, DePauw's scouting and preparation process for the Wabash game was completely acceptable by our standards at DePauw, AFCA, and NCAA rules and standards of conduct. It is also perfectly acceptable for coaches standing on their own sidelines to observe an opponent and relay those observations

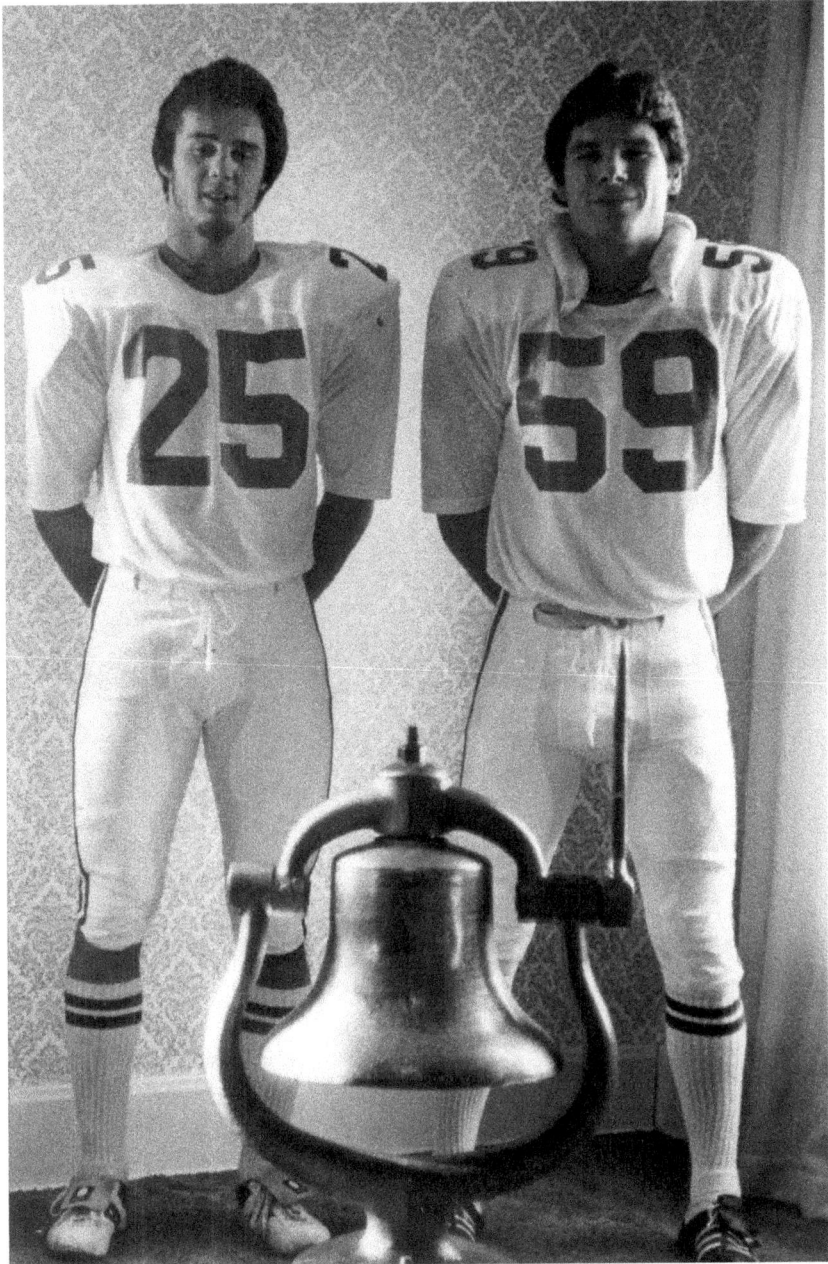

Randy Mellinger (25) and Bill Cannon (59) of Wabash pose with the Monon Bell in 1978, the year before the Little Giants lost in the national championship game against Widener. *Courtesy of DePauw Archives.*

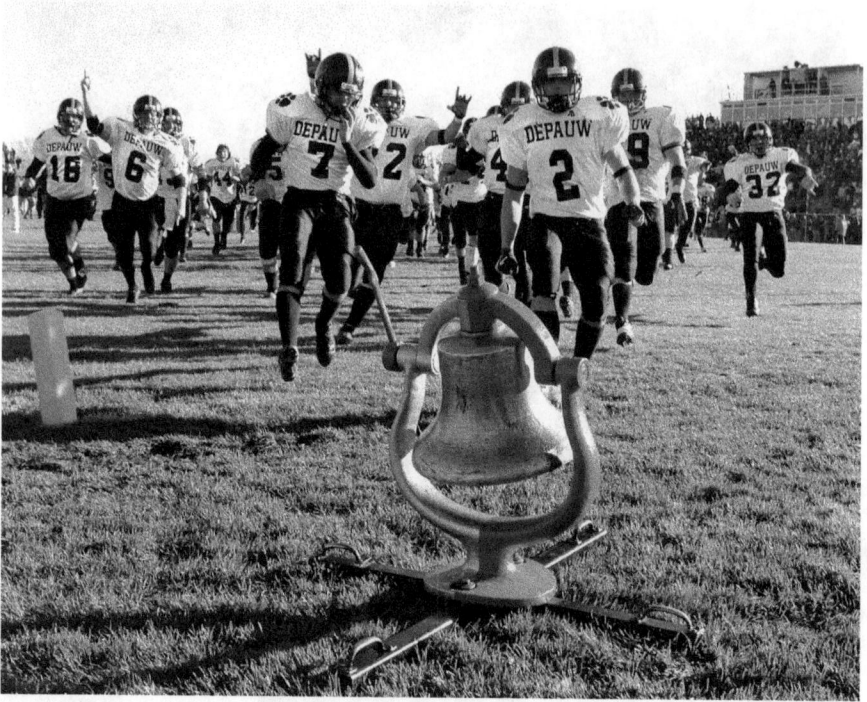

DePauw players rush to the Monon Bell following a 14–7 victory at Hollett Little Giant Stadium in 2004. *Courtesy of DePauw Archives.*

to their players, including what plays might be expected based on what an opponent is saying or signaling.

Mourouzis later closed his speech with a quote from the AFCA Code of Ethics that said a coach should set the example by "losing without bitterness." Days later, he heard from AFCA Ethics Committee Chair John Mackovic, former head coach at Illinois and Texas, that he was cleared of any wrongdoing. "We agree with you that no scouting rules were violated by DePauw," Mackovic's letter read in part. "There likely was some misunderstanding since both schools are in different conferences this year. We also agree that you did not violate any rules or ethics in detecting the signals for Wabash. As a committee, we strongly recommend that you and Coach Carlson get together prior to the season and have a complete understanding about scouting, video exchange, and any other items which may lead to misunderstandings. Your rivalry is to be cherished; do not lose its true meaning."

Carlson still questions the sportsmanship involved with stealing an opponent's signals.

> *"There was nothing in the Code of Ethics about it, but there is a strong statement about sportsmanship and character. I just wanted to see how they felt about it," Carlson said. "They were hands off with that. They were like, 'Wait a minute now. We're not going down that road.' They basically said you two schools, you two coaches, you have to work this out. You have to come to some kind of an agreement.*
>
> *"We learned a hard lesson that day, so we changed how we had plays called into the football game. We learned the hard way. Coach Mourouzis and I see each other every year at the AFCA convention. We talk. We're cordial. We're still professional friends. I'm not bitter at Nick and say I'll never talk to the guy again. He did what he felt he had to, and it wasn't against any particular NCAA rules.*

Carlson, 7-10-1 in Bell games, coached twice more against Mourouzis before Wabash looked for a new coach following the 2000 season. Mourouzis coached at DePauw through 2003 and finished with an 11-11-1 Bell record.

Chapter 6

1981: COACH NICK'S CREW BREAKS THROUGH

DEPAUW 21, WABASH 14

Blackstock Stadium didn't have enough seats. Two seating areas with a combined capacity of 4,000 provided less than half the necessary room for the 10,704 fans gathered for the 1981 regular season finale.

The eighty-eighth matchup between the Monon Bell rivals pitted a 9–0 Wabash squad against an 8–1 DePauw team. With the added stakes of a playoff bid and a perfect regular season for the Little Giants, local football fans flocked to Greencastle in droves. Fans without seats surrounded the field five or six people deep. Some looking for better views climbed trees next to the cemetery behind the Wabash sidelines. A game-time temperature of sixty-eight degrees was described as "utopian" in the official box score. Two giant "Ws" of dead grass scarred the turf in Greencastle, the result of a game-week prank from the Wabash faithful.

Set to start in his third Monon Bell game, DePauw quarterback Rob Doyle knew this game was different. He quarterbacked near-upsets the previous two years, but the setup for his final game as a senior felt bigger. "It was just amazing. It was an incredible atmosphere that day," Doyle said. "There was a sense that there were some really good teams and really good players on that field that actually got a chance in the NFL. The game was bigger. You walked out and you saw that."

Both programs reached a peak at the same time but took very different paths in the past five years to get there. Wabash College reached the Division III national championship, the Amos Alonzo Stagg Bowl, in 1977 and carried that momentum in the following years. That same year,

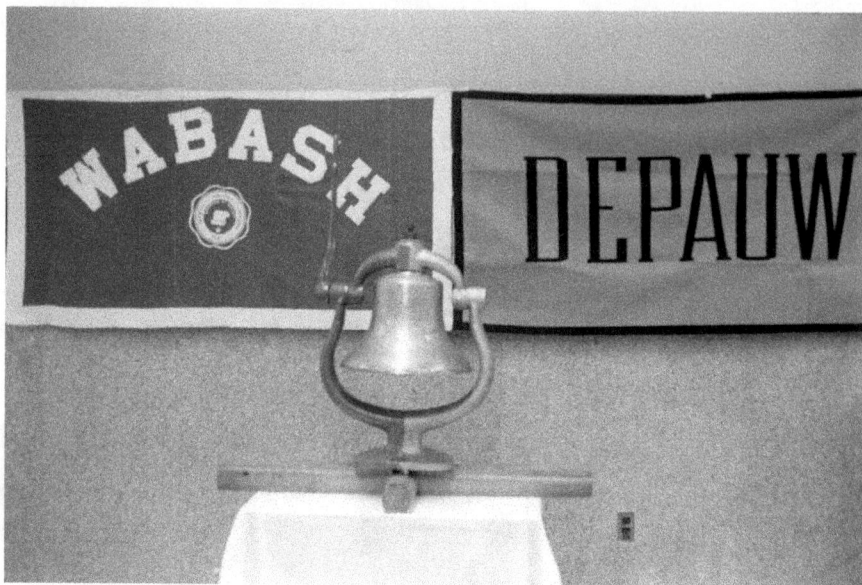

The Monon Bell on display with flags of its two annual suitors. *Courtesy of DePauw Archives.*

DePauw went through its first season without head coach Tom Mont in nearly two decades. As a result, the Tigers stumbled through a 1–9 season under Bob Bergman.

Four seasons later, Crawfordsville became a semi-permanent home for the Monon Bell. Two DePauw coaches failed to bring the Bell back to Greencastle, though some DePauw student thievery allowed it to make a couple appearances. A tie in 1980 marked DePauw's closest effort to return the Bell to its Old Gold home. By the time the '81 season finale came around, Wabash rolled off twenty-four consecutive games without a loss.

Alan Hill knew what all the fuss was about. He came to DePauw to join the track-and-field team in '77. After a year playing intramural football, he joined the varsity team for his first taste of the rivalry in '78. He didn't even have a grasp of all the rules of football at that point, let alone the importance of a Monon Bell matchup. Three years later, with his collegiate career coming to a close, Hill was anxious to finally ring that old locomotive dinger. "We were ready," Hill said. "It all sort of culminated in, 'This is us. This is our time. Let's make it happen.'"

Each DePauw senior was given a chance to speak to the team gathered in the locker room before the game. The speeches varied from motivational to hysterical, but the tension already started to erupt. A group that saw some of the darkest times in DePauw's football history had one last chance to redeem itself.

"We had a great group of seniors, and we just refused to lose that day," said senior running back Mark McConnell. "It was our fourth attempt without success, and I think we had just made up our minds that no matter what happened, when the game was over, we were going to be victorious."

MONTHS AFTER WABASH lost 39–36 to Widener University in the Division III national championship, Pete Metzelaars decided to join the Little Giants. A two-sport stud at Portage Central High School in Michigan, Metzelaars chose Wabash over Dartmouth College, Albion College and a couple Division II options in 1978. Crawfordsville was just far enough from home, and the Little Giants would allow him to play both football and basketball. That same year, Broad Ripple High School running back Daryl Johnson joined Wabash. Together the two became the core of future Little Giant offenses.

Assistant coach Stan Parrish received a promotion to head coach for the '78 season after Frank Navarro took the head coaching job at Princeton. Parrish encountered his first Monon Bell game the year before, but he already understood the weight of the rivalry on Wabash's campus. "Everybody was just wired into that game," Parrish said. "I think it was Frank Navarro who told me when I took over as head coach…he said just make sure you carry on with what we're doing and beat DePauw. It was just that simple. Nobody else has a game like that in small college."

Parrish successfully picked up right where Navarro left Wabash and completed an 8–1 season, capped with an 11–3 win over DePauw. The next season, Parrish, who would later coach Brian Griese, Tom Brady and Drew Henson at Michigan, found a quarterback to lead his offense.

Awarded a full-tuition Lilly Scholarship for academics, Carmel High School's Dave Broecker was brought into Wabash to compete for the starting quarterback position. He won the spot for the '79 season opener and started every game at Wabash for the next four seasons. "He came in, and from day one, you knew he was a special quarterback," said Metzelaars, a tight end. "He was just so accurate with the football. He made very quick, decisive decisions, sharp decisions, and the correct decisions almost all the time to deliver the ball and get it where it needed to be. He took charge of the huddle and was confident in himself and who he was as a player and a person."

As talented of an offensive trio as Wabash had ever seen, Broecker, Metzelaars and Johnson embarked on a three-year run that brought twenty-four wins and only two losses to the Little Giant program. But no matter how dominating a season Wabash was having, DePauw still managed to put up a fight as underdogs.

The Tigers let a win slip away in the 1979 game at Blackstock Stadium. A Rob Doyle touchdown early in the fourth quarter gave DePauw a 13–3 lead, but moments later, Wabash's Dave Kennedy returned a kickoff eighty-five yards to shift the tide. Broecker completed the comeback with a short touchdown run with less than three minutes remaining in the game for a 16–13 victory. After the game, one of the Wabash offensive linemen handed Broecker a towel he stole from a DePauw defensive lineman. Embroidered on the towel were the words "Destroy Broecker." Not exactly a warm welcome (but one to be expected) for a Little Giant quarterback making his first trip to DePauw's campus.

Somehow, the 1980 matchup proved to be even closer. DePauw scored the final points of the game, but it wasn't enough to earn a win. For the first time since 1959 and the eighth time to date, the Monon Bell Classic ended in a tie. With less than two minutes remaining, Doyle finished off an eighty-yard drive with a seventeen-yard touchdown pass to wide receiver Jay True to cut the score to 22–20. Another completion to True for the two-point conversion knotted the score. Despite DePauw's late efforts, the Bell would remain in Crawfordsville for another year.

"It just always seemed like maybe we didn't always play up to our potential and they played a little bit over their head," Metzelaars said. "That's kinda the feeling it was. They'd throw the ball, and we struggled playing defense against them. We didn't quite move the ball like we had been and could have and should have."

Wabash remained talented enough to hold off DePauw for five years straight, but the gap between rosters seemed to have closed.

The DePauw football program struggled to find both success and stability at the end of the 1970s. Tommy Mont's final season as head coach in 1976 marked the start of four straight seasons with no more than two wins. Mont, continuing to serve as athletic director, replaced himself with Bob Bergman, head coach at the Rose-Hulman Institute of Technology, in April of '77. His tenure ended after two floundering seasons with just three wins in nineteen games.

In 1979, the university tabbed Jerry Berndt, an assistant coach at Dartmouth College, to take over the program. Wins continued to elude the

Jerry Berndt led DePauw as head coach for the 1979 and 1980 seasons. Though he lost to and tied Wabash in his two Monon Bell Classics, he played a crucial role in turning around the Tiger program that beat the Little Giants in 1981 under head coach Nick Mourouzis. *Courtesy of DePauw Archives.*

Tigers in Berndt's first year, finishing 2–7 once again, but the new coach brought a different feel to the team.

"Jerry Berndt's a great coach," said quarterback Rob Doyle. "He really is one of the best coaches I've ever had. Bergman was a great recruiter, but they were floundering. Things were tough. Berndt came and just changed everything immediately. We went from really struggling to really playing well."

Practices were more organized, and after a year, Berndt and the Tigers started producing victories in the '80 season. DePauw opened the season with five wins before losses to Valparaiso University and St. Joseph's College leveled off the momentum. A season-ending tie with Wabash marked the state of the program perfectly: close, but not quite there yet. The problem was Berndt wasn't going to stick around to complete the turnaround. He jumped on an offer to become the head coach at the University of Pennsylvania and left the DePauw administration looking for a replacement for the third time in four years.

With an emphasis on finding a coach who would stick around, DePauw underwent an exhaustive search that included coaches familiar with the university but also coaches with Division I resumes looking for a place to settle. Returning senior captains Rob Doyle and Bob Torkelson were included in the process of interviewing coaches to sort through the right fit. Jim Gruden, recently let go as an assistant coach at the University of Notre Dame, and Nick Mourouzis, fresh off an assistant job at Northwestern University, were two of the favorites.

Mourouzis, who had already coached football for more than twenty years since finishing a football career at Miami University in Ohio, had a couple important influences favoring him. As Mourouzis tells it, a recommendation from Indiana University head basketball coach Bobby Knight helped his case. Mourouzis ran into Knight while evaluating a recruit at a basketball game at Glenbrook North High School, where Mourouzis's son attended school. Mourouzis approached Knight, and eventually the conversation led to his search for a job after the staff at Northwestern was let go. When Mourouzis mentioned DePauw, Knight said he knew the athletic director, Tommy Mont, and that he would give him a call. "Mont was impressed with that," Mourouzis said.

Mourouzis did more impressing during the interview process. "Nick came in and didn't have any of the formality," Doyle said. "He came in and started talking, got on the board and was diagramming his offense and the things we were going to do. He had a huge amount of enthusiasm. It wasn't for us to decide. They asked our opinion. I was like, there's your guy right there. He's been in the Big Ten. He's been on all the moves that you have to make in Division I. He wants a home. He wants a place where he can coach and build a program. I think he's here for the long term and for the university. I think he'd be great."

On February 17, 1981, DePauw announced Mourouzis as its new head football coach at a press conference in Indianapolis. He would soon make his first wise decision as a DePauw coach in retaining defensive assistant coaches Ted Katula and Tim Hreha. Both DePauw graduates, Katula and Hreha would provide a holdover for the upperclassmen who had already survived through plenty of coaching changes.

"Coach Nick's desire to keep them with the program and let them build the defense was big," said senior linebacker Bob Cathcart. "We were doing some things defensively from a scheme side that other people weren't doing. We had the athletes—especially Alan Hill in the back—that allowed us to do that."

By the time practice started in August, Mourouzis, who became known simply as "Coach Nick" to players wanting to avoid butchering his Greek last name, established a new feeling within the program. A player's coach, Mourouzis brought confidence and enthusiasm to his job.

"Our freshman year, it was not a good experience for a lot of us. But guys hung in there and got going," Cathcart said. "Jerry Berndt certainly made a difference when he came in with a level of a professionalism and attitude that the program needed. We were distressed when Jerry left, but the minute you got to meet Nick, you were like, 'Wow, OK. We're going to keep going right where we left off.' His expertise and positive attitude—everything that he did—was just taking it to another level from where Jerry brought it."

"Nick was a master at building off of what Jerry had started," said senior wide receiver Scott Welch. "He didn't come in with an ego that said, 'You're going to do it my way, and we're changing this.' He kept a lot of the offense in particular similar. He added nuances to it, but he didn't remodel it. I think that did a lot. Then he's such a real positive guy. He did a lot for our confidence and told us how good we were going to be."

Defensive back Alan Hill, who already excelled in track and field with a 1981 national championship in the pole vault, had one last football season to translate his athleticism into an elite football player. "I always said Bergman recruited me, Jerry Berndt coached me and Nick got the best out of me," Hill said. "That's really what it was."

The ceiling for the '81 DePauw squad hadn't been defined, but with a core unit of seniors returning from a 7–2 season the year before, the Tigers had the pieces in place to make a special run. In the first game of the season, one of the first preseason coaching decisions paid off. Hill, who was moved from cornerback the previous season to safety, intercepted four passes in a 31–7 victory over St. Norbert College. Mourouzis's offense clicked the following week in a 35–21 win over Hope College.

Hreha and Meyer welcomed the increased scoring with open arms. No longer did they have to play near-perfect defense in order to stay in games. Mourouzis started a routine of predicting how many plays it would take for the offense to score. "He would always say, 'We're going to score in five' or 'We're going to score in six.' Coach Meyer and I were looking at each other [and remembering] there were games we were hoping for just one score in previous years," Hreha said. "We're looking at him and going, 'You gotta be kidding.' And eventually they ended up scoring in six. He was very inventive offensively. It really took a lot of pressure off the defense most of the time."

Both sides of the ball felt the pressure of the season's biggest challenge in week three. DePauw headed to Ohio to play the University of Dayton, defending national champions in Division III. Playing in front of a crowd of twelve thousand fans on an Astroturf field only added to the challenges the Flyers presented against DePauw. The Tigers hung close but fell by a score of 16–0 for the first loss of the season. Missed opportunities, including costly penalties like the one that nullified a fifty-eight-yard return touchdown on an interception late in the fourth quarter, cost the Tigers the game.

Feeling that the game had slipped away, the Tigers hoped they would earn a chance at a rematch in the playoffs. "We knew we were going to win the rest of the way," Hill said. "A lot of the time I was focusing on getting to play Dayton again. That was just our mindset. We're going to play them again, and we're going to beat them."

Wins in the next six games of the season kept the slim hope of a Dayton rematch alive. All that remained was Mourouzis's first Monon Bell Classic against an 8–0 Wabash team with a 258–73 aggregate against opposing teams. The first-year head coach instilled a confidence in his team that expected nothing less than a victory against its rival. "By the time we got to the Monon Bell game," said senior running back Mark McConnell, "we wanted to win it for him just as bad as we did for ourselves."

THE MORNING OF HIS FINAL Monon Bell game, DePauw quarterback Rob Doyle noticed a piece of mail waiting for him at breakfast. Inside the envelope, Doyle found a red Wabash bumper sticker with the slogan "Foil Doyle." In case he needed the reminder, the clever rhyming hinted at Wabash's determination in defeating the senior quarterback one last time and ending his career without a Monon Bell victory.

Doyle and the rest of the senior class had their own regrets from their previous encounters with Wabash. The last time the Little Giants made a trip to Blackstock Stadium, they left with a comeback victory in 1979.

Linebacker Bob Torkelson remembered the pain and learned from the mistakes made as a sophomore. "That was evidence of the fact that a lot of the people that were playing in that game were still sophomores," Torkelson said. "It was one of those situations where I think we had it and then the emotions kind of took over. They had a really good team. Wabash always put a good team on the field. They came from behind, and it slipped through our fingers."

Fellow linebacker Bob Cathcart couldn't quite get his fingers on one Wabash completion in the '79 game, and the thoughts of "what if" still lingered. "Wabash, more than anybody else, we probably had more preparation, more film, more study, more everything to get ready for knowing what their tendencies were," Cathcart said. "I missed a play on the ball by less than a foot that would have changed the game. That one I remember clearly, and it will probably haunt me forever."

Focused on finally putting an end to the frustration, the Tigers came out to start the game looking more like the team that hadn't beaten Wabash since 1975. The emotions brewing in the locker room spilled onto the field, where the 10,704 fans greeted both teams. Unfortunately for DePauw, the hype mismanaged to start the game.

The Wabash offense tested a normally reliable DePauw defense from the opening kickoff. The first ten plays from scrimmage saw the Little Giants travel sixty-one yards down to the DePauw two-yard line. Thirty-eight rushing yards for running back Daryl Johnson and seventeen passing yards and six rushing yards from quarterback Dave Broecker put Wabash on the doorstep of an early lead.

"There becomes a time when you're almost over-hyped for a game," Cathcart said. "For us seniors, it was a very emotional time in the locker room before the game, our last game. That last game for the seniors, the locker room tends to be very emotional. I think we kinda wore ourselves out a little bit coming into that game. They were ready for us and took it to us."

However, the Tiger defense stood tall on the goal line. Two runs to the right from Johnson were stuffed, and a Broecker incompletion brought on the field-goal team. Frank Kolisek set up for a twenty-two-yard attempt, but DePauw's Alan Hill snuck around the left side of the Wabash line and blocked the kick.

"We fell into a very predictable pattern and became probably a little bit too conservative getting down on the goal line like that," Broecker said. A pair of isolation runs by Johnson was exactly what the Little Giants were expected to do in short yardage situations. "If I had it to do all over again, I probably would have just called a quarterback sneak and scored that way. But hindsight is twenty-twenty. DePauw stopped us on our opening drive. We went all the way down to the two-yard line, and that was a big momentum shift. It proved to DePauw that they could play with us."

DePauw head coach Nick Mourouzis responded with aggressive play-calling for his offense's first series. Seven of the first nine plays for the Tigers were Doyle pass attempts. Thirty-five yards into a promising drive, the passing attack backfired. One play after the Wabash secondary missed an opportunity for an interception, Doyle followed up with another errant throw, this time landing in the hands of defensive back David Rogers for a turnover.

Rebounding from its last stalled drive, the Wabash offense relied on Broecker and Johnson to move the ball down the field once again. Three complete passes and three running plays left the Little Giants with a third-and-eleven at the DePauw sixteen-yard line. Broecker swung the third-down pass to the left to Johnson, who scurried up the field for twelve yards and a first down. On the next play, Johnson took a toss left and powered his way into the end zone. A Kolisek extra point gave Wabash a 7–0 lead with one minute and fifteen seconds remaining in the first quarter.

Facing a deficit, the Tigers still relied on Rob Doyle's right arm to stay in the game. On third-and-seven from his own forty-six, Doyle unleashed a bomb down the left side of the field to senior wide receiver Scott Welch. The ball traveled fifty yards in the air until it fell perfectly into the arms of the Tiger receiver draped by two Wabash defenders. Tackled at the six-yard line, Welch put the Tigers in a scoring position in the final seconds of the first quarter. Two plays later, on the first snap of the second quarter, Doyle threw for DePauw's first score of the game. Senior wide receiver Kevin Perkins started wide right and motioned closer to the middle of the field before the snap. Crossing the field while drifting toward the back of the end zone, Perkins kept his defender behind him to allow Doyle to loft a throw in his direction in the end zone. The dynamic receiver leaped and caught the ball with fully extended arms over his head to pull in the touchdown. Doyle missed a wide-open Bob Cohen in the back corner of the end zone, but nonetheless the Tigers tied the game at seven with the addition of Dave Finzer's extra point.

"I wasn't wide open. I was open enough," Perkins said. "Robby had enough confidence in me to throw it up high and know that I'm going to go up there and get it. That's what happened. It was a high pass. It was in the very back of the end zone right off to the left of the upright. I hauled it in and made sure I got both feet in before [Wabash defender] Tony Will pushed me out of bounds."

Perkins had been hobbled all week after getting his foot stepped on the week before against Maryville College. Limited in practice, he had a special insert made for his cleats by team doctor Mark Stevens to protect his injured right foot. He was unable to push off his right leg with the same force as normal, but the motivation of winning the Monon Bell was enough of a pain reliever to help him push through. "I'm sitting on the sideline, and I heard that bell ringing when Johnson scored," Perkins said. "I'm like, 'Well, this is bullshit. We're going to have to drive the field, and we're going to have to freaking score.' That was our mentality. I know that was going through everybody's mind on offense."

On the ensuing kickoff, the Wabash front line took a hit when senior offensive guard Chris Carr crumpled to the ground during the kickoff return. Carr received medical attention (he later learned he tore his MCL) but insisted he walk off on his own. Four years prior, Carr sat inside Blackstock Stadium watching the 1977 Monon Bell Classic as a DePauw recruit with his father, Bob, a 1959 Wabash graduate, who was naturally cheering for his alma mater. When Wabash expressed interest later that year, Carr chose to follow his father's legacy.

Relegated to the sideline for his final college game, Carr argued his case to the training staff to be allowed to return. It was a battle that Carr couldn't win. The pain slowly set in as the game went on, and the Wabash offensive attack was forced to continue without Carr.

A Metzelaars fumble and a missed fifty-two-yard field goal by Finzer ended the following Wabash and DePauw drives. Then the Little Giants returned to efficiently moving the ball down the field once again, with every single yard attributed to the offensive power trio of Broecker, Metzelaars and Johnson. Working as a quarterback catalyst, Broecker ran four times for forty-five yards and completed a fourteen-yard pass to Metzelaars. Johnson chipped in with eleven rushing yards of his own, the final nine coming on a touchdown run to give his team the lead once again. Broecker pitched the ball on an option right before getting hit by two DePauw defenders, and Johnson eluded one would-be tackler in a race to the end zone. A Kolisek extra point gave the Little Giants a 14–7 lead with seven minutes and fifty-six seconds left in the first half.

Johnson grew to know a number of the Tiger defenders throughout the years. He took plenty of shots from linebackers Cathcart and Torkelson, but he had triumphs of his own, like the two touchdown runs in the first half. "They probably knew some of my tendencies, and I probably knew some of theirs. That never came into mind when you got on the field, because you're looking to win," Johnson said. "I'm trying to run past them, and they're trying to catch me. A few times they got a few good hits on me, but normally I got away from them before they could get a good hit on me."

Surrendering fourteen points in less than two quarters, DePauw's defense was ceding points to an opposing offense at a higher rate than at any point throughout the season. The unit hadn't allowed three touchdowns in a game since the second week of the season against Hope College, and all three of those scores came in a fourth-quarter comeback attempt when reserve players entered the lineup. Needing to keep up with the Little Giants, the Tiger offense slowed down the tempo of the game. Starting at its own twenty-yard line, DePauw ran the ball on the first four plays of the drive for fifteen yards. Two Doyle completions moved the Tigers into Little Giant territory before the attack returned to the ground. Rick Lindlow and Rich Bonaccorsi combined for forty-eight yards on eleven carries to move the Old Gold offense to the five-yard line.

The clock ran down to under two minutes, and the Tigers were hoping to knot the score at fourteen before halftime. On third-and-goal, Doyle lofted a pass to the left back corner of the end zone for Perkins. A good defensive play, which didn't always stop Perkins, forced an incompletion and left DePauw with fourth down. But instead of sending out the field-goal unit, Mourouzis elected to go for the touchdown once more. He wanted to try the fade again. "I was young and aggressive and thought, 'Let's go after it,'" Mourouzis said. "I had confidence in that fade route."

So did Doyle and Perkins. "To me, that was money," Doyle said. "That play was going to be successful. There was no question that he'd come down with it. I don't think I made a good throw the first time. Coming back to it, we weren't going to miss it twice."

Taking the snap at the right hash, Doyle dropped back three steps and quickly arched a ball toward the back corner of the end zone on the left side before Perkins even crossed the goal line. The six-foot-three Perkins ran hard into the end zone but stopped at the last second, shielding his defender off and squaring up to the ball, headed right to him. The two made the play look effortless.

A Finzer extra point tied the game at fourteen with one minute and nineteen seconds left before halftime. As the time ran out, both teams headed to their locker rooms in the middle of a stalemate. The quarterback-and-receiver combo delivered the points for the Tigers, but Mourouzis delivered a message to his team. They weren't going to back down to the undefeated Little Giants.

"At halftime, you just have a different attitude having another seven points under your belt," Welch said. "Kevin Perkins was just a great athlete. It did a lot to set the stage for our whole second-half strategy. It would have been a lot more defensive if it was, 'Well, let's just kick a field goal, guys.' It showed that we were there to win."

DEPAUW ASSISTANT COACH Tim Hreha walked around the locker room and shook hands with his defensive players. Instilling confidence in a defense that didn't resemble itself in the first half, Hreha congratulated every player. He might not get the chance to in the chaos following a victory, he told them.

Senior linebacker Bob Torkelson would be one of the key players counted on to turn that confidence into a productive second half. "We all felt like we were capable of doing that. Once halftime came and went, we really felt that we were going to be there," Torkelson said. "Not cockiness, but there was a feeling of confidence in the locker room that we were going to be able continue to do what we were doing. The offense had continued moving the ball, and we had tightened up to be able to hold them."

"We had this weird confidence," said sophomore linebacker Marshall Reavis. "If you looked in Torkleson's or Cathcart's eyes, I just felt we were going to win the game almost the entire time during it. They score, and it's alright—we've got a great offense."

The scoreboard showed a tie game, but the halftime box score favored the visiting team. Wabash gained more yards (240) than DePauw (179) in the first half and tallied five more first downs. Little Giant running back Daryl Johnson ran for 81 yards, and quarterback Dave Broecker added 65 rushing yards of his own to complement his 94 yards passing. Despite his fumble, Wabash tight end Pete Metzelaars also put together a solid first half with five catches for 48 yards. The Tigers set out to limit the power trio for Wabash in the last thirty minutes. "To some degree, they were pushing us around a little bit," said DPU linebacker Bob Cathcart. "And they just didn't do that in the second half."

After a DePauw punt, the Tiger defense had its first chance to assert itself in the second half. The Scarlet offense picked up thirty-nine yards in four plays, but the defense took advantage of another Wabash fumble on the fifth play. Sprinting through an opening on the right side of the offense, Johnson appeared on his way for a big gain, but defensive back Kurt Jones reached out, knocked the ball out of his arms and recovered the fumble. If Jones hadn't hit the ball, Johnson might have bounced off the tackle attempt and scampered for a long touchdown.

The DePauw offense responded with a drive similar to the one that tied the game late in the second quarter. A heavy dosage of run mixed with a few passes when necessary chewed time off the clock as the Tigers matriculated down the field. Thirteen plays (eight running, five passing) moved the ball from DePauw's own thirty-three-yard line to the Wabash eight. On second-and-seven, Mourouzis called for the same fade route to wide receiver Kevin Perkins that worked earlier. Well defended, Perkins could not get in position to make a play on the throw from Doyle. To end a drive propelled by outworking the Little Giants, Mourouzis chose a play, 54 R Read, to outsmart the defense on third down. The play revolved around a running back making a decision on his route depending on how the defense guarded him. Senior Mark McConnell was asked to carry out the play.

Fighting through a hip injury, McConnell knew he would be faced with a tough decision when choosing his route option. Earlier in the game, McConnell avoided cutting left, which would have aggravated his injury, even when the defense dictated that he should have. But faced with the final twenty minutes of his DePauw career, McConnell told himself he'd follow through with the correct read this time. "It didn't matter how bad it hurt, I was going to make the right decision," McConnell said. "Wherever the linebacker went, I was going to go the other way. Thank God the linebacker the second time around went in so I got to turn to my right and it wasn't painful. The ball was delivered, and the rest is history, so to speak."

McConnell crossed the line of scrimmage and found three defenders sucking into the middle of the field. He cut to his right a few yards down field with no white jerseys within ten yards of him. He caught the ball and scored untouched. The third Finzer extra point of the day gave DePauw its first lead at 21–14 with four minutes and twenty-two seconds left in the third quarter.

"Coach Nick deserves a lot of credit because it was a great play call," McConnell said. "As far as my part in it, I was pretty much a bit player or a role player. I was blessed that Coach Nick had the confidence in me to call a play that left me open. It was really just easy pitch and catch at that point."

A dominating performance from the DePauw defense to close the game allowed McConnell's touchdown to be the game-winning score. "I had no idea that would be the last touchdown scored. I don't think anybody did. We all felt there would be more scoring so I would be a footnote, not the one that caught what proved to be the winning touchdown," McConnell said. "I never felt totally confident until the game was over. I wasn't going to celebrate early or assume that we had it in the bag. Everybody was that way after being snake-bitten for three years before that. Everybody was going to play hard until it was over."

Four Wabash drives to end the game resulted in zero points. Only one drive, early in the fourth quarter, saw the Little Giants cross the fifty-yard line. That drive ended in a thirty-seven-yard yard missed field goal by Frank Kolisek. On the last offensive play of the game for Wabash, Broecker scrambled to avoid the DePauw pass rush but could only find Johnson a few yards down the field. The DPU defense held one last time to allow Doyle and the offense to run out the clock. The Old Gold won the Monon Bell for the first time in six years.

"We hadn't tasted the Bell," said senior safety Alan Hill. "The first thought was the feeling of excitement. That was unbelievable. Then we ran over there and tried to pick it up and I thought, 'Man, this thing is heavy.' I was exhausted, so I thought I'd let these other guys carry it. It was just unbelievable. All the hard work had paid off."

THE MISSED OPPORTUNITIES still haunt members of that 1981 Wabash team. Daryl Johnson and Pete Metzelaars each have fumbles etched into their brains. It's even wiped away some of the good memories from that '81 season for Johnson. "You don't care about the rest of the season when that particular game is what you want to win. To walk out of the stadium that particular day and lose, that's a heartbreaker," Johnson said. "I don't think you ever forget it. Even now—I'm fifty-three—boy I wish I could go back out there and play again and do that play over again. It stays with you."

Chris Carr didn't even have the chance to finish what he started. With a mangled knee, his sideline view couldn't have been any worse. Years later, Carr, a sports psychologist, returned to Blackstock Stadium to the spot where his football career ended. It was a way to help heal the wounds left from his Monon Bell finale. "It was always complicated because I was a bit envious of the guys even though we lost," Carr said. "But they got to finish playing on the field. I remember very vividly the game ending. At this point, I'm pretty sore and my knee's not very mobile, so I'm not walking too well. I just remember that sick feeling I had."

Stan Parrish might have left Wabash following the '81 season, but he couldn't bring himself to ditch the Little Giants after that heartbreaking loss. "When I lost that game and we rode back on the bus, I didn't care who I had coming back. I was not leaving losing to DePauw." He'd return with Dave Broecker as his quarterback for one more year to beat DePauw in 1982. Parrish left for Purdue University the following year.

"That was actually the low point of my four years at Wabash," Broecker said. "Getting beat in the game, ruining the perfect season, ending the twenty-four-game unbeaten streak, losing the Monon Bell and knocking us out of the playoffs. Some of those seniors—Pete Metzelaars, Daryl Johnson and Chris Carr—they had been instrumental in helping us achieve that twenty-four-game streak. We knew that if we won that game, there was no way we weren't going to go the playoffs, because we were ranked very highly. But we didn't win that game, and we knew that was the end of it."

For DePauw, the celebration dragged on. They didn't know yet that they wouldn't receive one of the eight playoff bids and that their season was finished as well. Instead, they received a gift from DePauw president Richard Rosser. After he entered the locker room to congratulate the team, the players started to coax him to give them the day off on Monday. He caved to the players' request. "Everybody just started screaming, 'No school Monday! No school Monday!'" Bob Torkelson said. "I think he felt like he had to give us a day off Monday or he wasn't going to get out of there."

Speaking with reporters after his first Monon Bell game, Nick Mourouzis didn't shy away from the hyperbole. His coaching days in the Big Ten had passed, but he found a similar excitement in Greencastle, Indiana. He'd remain as the head coach at DePauw for twenty-three years, chasing that same feeling at the end of every season. "This is probably the third biggest moment in my life," Mourouzis told *The DePauw*. "The first was when I got married, the second when I was at IU and we won to go to the Rose Bowl, and now this."

Chapter 7

1986: A SHIFT FROM HOUSE

WABASH 24, DEPAUW 23

Bill Kaiser's legacy came with a lot of bruises. In the 1985 matchup between DePauw and Wabash, Kaiser carried a heavy load for the Little Giants. Fifty eight times the junior running back from Jasper, Indiana, was asked to carry the football for Wabash's offense. Setting a Division III record for carries in a game, Kaiser racked up 211 yards in a 28–8 Monon Bell victory. He stamped his mark on the rivalry, and the rivalry repaid him with some black-and-blue body parts. At one point, Kaiser carried the ball on twenty-three consecutive offensive plays for Wabash. He became friends with an oxygen machine at halftime trying to catch his breath. The bruises would settle in later, and a broken finger would have an entire offseason to heal. After getting his hand stuck in a defender's facemask, he ran quickly to the sideline between plays to have a trainer tape the injured finger to a healthy one. He remained in the game, and Wabash scored a touchdown on the next play.

The 1986 season brought new challenges for Kaiser. Defenses knew stopping the record-setting running back was the key to limiting the Little Giants, especially the rivals down in Greencastle. After the '85 campaign resulted in 1,465 yards for Kaiser, he was held to just 638 yards through the first eight games of the '86 season. Certainly the DePauw Tiger defense would be hell-bent on shutting down Kaiser as a senior in the ninety-third Monon Bell Classic. "That happened all year. After that point, I had a big target on my back," Kaiser said. "There were other things that we had to do. One thing about Division III football is there are always a lot of guys that can step up and do different things. People come out and have great games."

The Monon Bell and the old Monon Railroad. *Courtesy of DePauw Archives.*

Wabash head coach Greg Carlson made sure Kaiser had plenty of talent surrounding him. In his fourth year as head coach, Carlson started to become an expert at recruiting successful high school athletes to come to an all-male institution. "You never went into a high school to talk to a young man who projected himself in an all-male collegiate setting," Carlson said. "There aren't high school juniors in Indiana that say, 'Boy, I can't wait to go to an all-male school when I get out of high school.' The biggest factor for Wabash was its academic reputation. People knew that guys that graduated from Wabash were going on to achieve great things in their professional careers."

Still, the 1986 Little Giants struggled through the season, at least in comparison to recent program success. With a 5–3 record entering the Monon Bell Classic, they became only the third Wabash team to lose three games in a season in the previous decade. In order to win a third straight Bell game, the team needed to embody the school motto birthed by a pair of alums in 1919: "Wabash Always Fights."

The offense, featuring Kaiser at running back, Curt Selby at quarterback and Tom Vandergriff at wide receiver, struggled and set a modern-day school record for fewest total yards in a season: 2,208. Linebacker Jay Herrmann and cornerback Marty Kaiser, Bill's younger brother, led the defensive efforts of the team.

"People knew what was coming. We were not offensively successful," Bill Kaiser said. "There were some other guys that came through. That's the great thing about the Bell game. People sometimes surpass what their expected athletic skill level is and do big things."

Only time would tell which Little Giants stood tallest.

A SCORELESS FIRST QUARTER played right into the hands of Wabash. DePauw's offense, led by quarterback Jeff Voris, presented nary a threat of scoring in the first fifteen minutes. A unit averaging 23.4 points per game was held scoreless in the first quarter. The leg of Tom Downham was needed to start the scoring in the second stanza. Three straight DePauw drives ended in Downham field goals of thirty, thirty-five and twenty-one yards. Meanwhile, the Wabash offense was limited to just twelve plays in the second quarter. Little Giant running back Bill Kaiser rushed for a measly twenty yards on eleven carries in the first half, and quarterback Curt Selby threw incomplete passes on all four attempts. One pass did land in a pair of hands, but those belonged to an intercepting DePauw defender.

The Tiger offense tallied 192 total yards of offense in the first half compared to 15 for Wabash but had only a 9–0 lead to show for it. Voris, who transferred to DePauw for the 1986 season after a redshirt freshman season at Division 1-AA Southwest Missouri State, knew his offense should have scored more points in the first half. "We kicked a lot of field goals when we should have scored touchdowns," Voris said. "You always look back... and you kick yourself for a couple passes that get away from you. You felt like you could have done more. We left some points on the board. In that game...it's a sixty-minute game, and guys are going to keep playing."

In the second half, Wabash's offense finally showed some life after a Jim Hebert fumble was recovered by the Little Giant defense. Selby and the Wabash offense started the drive at the DePauw thirty-two-yard line. An eleven-yard completion to wide receiver Tom Vandergriff followed by a defensive holding penalty put the Little Giants in a first-and-goal situation. A nine-yard Selby pass to Vandergriff resulted in the first score of the game for Wabash. The Little Giant offense awoke to trail 9–7 after a dreadful first half.

Voris halted the momentum shift on the ensuing drive. A forty-nine-yard completion to senior wide receiver Doug Penn quieted the Wabash faithful in Crawfordsville. Two plays later, the two connected again and stretched

Even the DePauw and Wabash mascots quarrel over the possession of the Monon Bell. *Courtesy of DePauw Archives.*

the lead back to nine points. Both teams scored their first touchdowns in a span of two minutes and thirteen seconds.

Another failed offensive possession gave the ball right back to Voris and Co. The Tiger offense moved down to the Wabash twenty-yard line following a thirty-six-yard pass from Voris to Hebert. Five plays later, Voris threw for his second touchdown of the game. Tim Weaver hauled in the nine-yard touchdown pass; Downham knocked in another extra point, and four minutes and thirteen seconds later, the game headed to the fourth quarter with the Tigers leading 23–7. The visitors were threatening to blow out Wabash in Little Giant Stadium. The home team needed a special final quarter.

KELLEY HOUSE FIRST IMAGINED what playing in a Monon Bell game would be like when he attended one as an eleven-year-old Crawfordsville resident. A couple years later, his father, Steve House, joined the Wabash football staff as a volunteer assistant coach. It was only a matter of time before Kelley House became a Little Giant. Following graduation from nearby Southmont High School, House enrolled at Wabash in the fall of 1986 to take his turn at the historic college football rivalry.

As a freshman, House started to learn about the traditions that ruled the Wabash campus in the weeks leading up to the Monon Bell Classic. Suddenly the rivalry became more than a heated football game every November. As a fraternity pledge, House spent part of his week protecting the Crawfordsville campus from DePauw intruders, adding security to his academic and athletic responsibilities for the week. "To be honest, that sucked for us," House said. "For me especially, because you've got this huge game, basically the biggest game of the year for you, coming up and during a critical practice week I'm sitting there with a winter coat on hovered next to a fire watching for DePauw guys to vandalize the campus or do whatever."

Because Wabash students put so much time into keeping the campus and the Monon Bell safe, the clang of the bell could be heard throughout campus during every reasonable hour of the day. The pride of the possession of the Monon Bell became apparent to anyone within ear's reach that week.

On the football team, House found his way onto the field as a special-teams player. He practiced all week looking forward to seeing action in his first Monon Bell game but learned Thursday that he might not get a chance. That's when Wabash head coach Greg Carlson posted the depth chart for the weekend.

House scanned the list looking for his name in the usual places. With a personal preference for the kickoff team, House looked to see where he was slated to line up but didn't see his named listed as one of the eleven starters. He continued to look at other special-teams unit and grew concerned. He asked one of his older teammates, who revealed that Carlson always plays upperclassmen on the special-teams units for the Bell game. Only one unit listed House's name: Tiger Return. "I was super bummed out," House said. "It's like a guy vying for a starting spot and realize he's not going to be playing," House said. "We practiced Tiger Return later that day, and I dealt with it. Come to find out Tiger Return was a punt block."

A 23–7 deficit in the fourth quarter eventually forced House onto the field that Saturday. The Little Giants needed to find a way to spark a comeback, and a DePauw fourth down on its own fourteen-yard line presented an opportunity. The Tiger Return team headed onto the field to try to block the punt. House, a 180-pound defensive back, lined up across from the long snapper with the shortest distance of any Little Giant between him and DePauw punter Michael Ehlers. "I'm over the ball with adrenaline just beyond anything you can imagine," House said. "I remember saying, 'As soon as that ball moves, I'm off.'"

On the snap, House used a swim move to pass by the long snapper. A punt protector took out House below the waist, but his momentum projected him into the air. Falling toward Ehlers, House reached out for the ball. "I actually hit the ground, and then I heard the crowd. I wasn't sure what happened, but I heard this huge roar," House said. "It was an awesome sound." The ball ricocheted off House's helmet back into DePauw's end zone, where Marty Kaiser gathered the football for a Wabash touchdown.

"When I hit the ground, I looked up and saw the ball go off to the right, and I realized I had gotten it. I got it with my helmet," House said. "That's why I wasn't sure that I got it. I didn't really feel it."

In the press box, assistant coach Steve House watched his son shift the momentum of a Monon Bell game. He didn't have to hide his excitement. He celebrated with the other Wabash coaches watching the game from their perched view. "It was definitely a bookmark for me as a coach," Steve House said.

Trailing 23–14 with thirteen minutes and sixteen seconds left in the game, the Little Giants showed signs of life. The momentum shift continued at the other end of the field when DePauw kicker Tom Downham missed a thirty-eight-yard field goal attempt to close a promising drive for the Tigers. Then Curt Selby flexed his throwing arm to orchestrate a crucial drive for Wabash. Following a thirteen-yard run by Rich Riddle to start the drive, Selby threw two incompletions, but the second drew a fifteen-yard pass interference penalty on the Tiger defense. Three Selby completions in the next four plays combined for forty-four yards and put the Little Giants on the three-yard line. Running back Bill Kaiser, looking to finally break through like he was able to the year before, crashed through the line on first down for a touchdown. Another Tim Pliske extra point made the score 23–21, still in DePauw's favor.

Pliske's leg would be needed again shortly.

Tim Pliske stood on the field of Little Giant Stadium that Saturday long before most. His teammates were still in the locker room going through pregame rituals. Most fans were still in the parking lots loosening their vocal chords. Pliske and his fellow specialists went through their own pregame routine as the distractions started to fill into the stadium.

"You were out there doing pregame warm-ups as the first group. The quarterbacks didn't come out. The linemen didn't come out. You were out there early," Pliske said. "You pay attention, and you have to be a very focused to be able to do that, but you're aware of everything setting up. People are coming in. The band is starting to play. You really were able to catch the game from start to finish for an entire Saturday afternoon."

Few paid attention to Pliske knocking through field goals before the game, but all eyes would focus on him in the final minutes. A twenty-five-yard Michael Ehlers punt gave Wabash the ball at the DePauw thirty-two-yard line with two minutes and forty-eight seconds left in the game. The Little Giants were virtually within Pliske's range already with a two-point deficit.

Pliske knew his services might be needed, so he headed to the practice net on the sideline to loosen his leg one final time. As if he needed a reminder, nervous teammates approached the sophomore kicker making sure he understood the situation. He could no longer avoid the attention. "Everybody was coming up to me and saying, 'Hey, we're getting there. Hey, we're going to need you. Hey, you ready?' You really don't want to deal with them, but it does bring that awareness to you," Pliske said of the growing anticipation. "That's when you get a sense. Everybody else feels it, too."

When the Wabash drive stalled at the seventeen-yard line, Pliske was called on for a thirty-four-yard attempt on fourth down. But as Pliske awaited the snap, he wasn't the one to flinch. DePauw's defense jumped offside to move the ball five yards closer to the crossbar. Pliske had to reset and refocus.

"If they throw you off just a hair or you're thinking about something else, you're going to miss it. You're going to make a mistake," Pliske said. "It was just having to stop and start over. Beyond that, it was being a creature of habit: put the tee down, count off your steps and nod to your holder when you're ready. It's just routine, routine, routine."

On the snap of the ball, the kick looked the same as many other Pliske field goals. The left-footed kicker swung through the ball, and it sailed right down the middle of the uprights. Teammates hugged Pliske in celebration hoping his kick clinched another year of the Monon Bell in Crawfordsville. DePauw had one minute and six seconds left to prevent that from being the case.

Jeff Voris bounced around in the pocket trying to move his team down the field and create a chance to regain the lead in the final minute. The Tiger quarterback found wide receiver Tom Evans on first down for a twenty-yard gain to move the Tigers out to their own forty-two-yard line. A ten-yard penalty on Wabash and another twenty-yard completion to Evans gave DePauw a clearer view of the end zone from the twenty-eight-yard line. Two incompletions followed and left the Tigers with a third-and-ten with just twenty-five seconds left.

Wabash linebacker Jay Herrmann tried to calm his fellow defenders as they continued to cede yards to Voris and his receiving targets. "We were like a big rubber band that was stretching," Herrmann said. "We

Above: Head coach Nick Mourouzis stayed at DePauw for twenty-three seasons, winning the Monon Bell Classic eleven times, losing eleven times and tying once. *Courtesy of DePauw Archives.*

Left: The Monon Bell sits on the Wabash sideline at Blackstock Stadium for the 1985 Monon Bell Classic. *Courtesy of DePauw Archives.*

Opposite: The DePauw team huddles before the 100th Monon Bell Classic in 1993. Wabash won the game 40–26 to give itself a 46–45–9 advantage in the historic series. *Courtesy of DePauw Archives.*

knew we were probably going to bend, but we were hoping we weren't going to break."

Little Giant quarterback Curt Selby could only watch from the sidelines. "I specifically remember saying all we needed to do was tackle somebody—get a sack," Selby said. "The best thing that could have happened would have been if they completed a pass and we tackled them. I don't know who I was standing with, but we were very clear that they didn't have any timeouts left."

Taking the shotgun snap, Voris dropped back scanning his options to the left, to the right and back to the middle of the field, where he found Greg Werner. Voris released the pass, and the sophomore tight end came back to catch the ball at the twenty-one-yard line. He surged forward but was corralled by a trio of Wabash defenders including Herrmann. The referees ruled Werner down at the nineteen-yard line, just short of a first down. "We thought we had the first down," said DePauw assistant coach Tim Hreha. Looking down from the press box, Hreha could only listen in on the conversation head coach Nick Mourouzis was having with his players on the sideline through a headset. "I remember him saying, 'First down. First down.' He turned to call the play, and the kids looked at him and said, 'No, coach. They're marking it short.' Now we're screaming, 'Field goal! Field goal! Field goal!' And all that time the clock is running."

Tom Downham and parts of the field-goal unit ran out onto the field hoping to get set for a field goal attempt with the clock ticking down to less than ten seconds. Confusion reigned as the clock melted away to zero. Fourteen DePauw players were on different parts of the field as time expired. Downham, waiting behind a scrambling line, raised his hands to his helmet in despair, and the Wabash sideline flooded onto the field.

"It was chaos at the end. You could tell they were scrambling to try to quickly line up," Herrmann said. "It was one of those things where literally they were at the line when the time ran out. It happened so quickly. The next thing you know, the game's over."

Wabash head coach Greg Carlson smiled from the sidelines. "From a Wabash standpoint, it was kinda comical. I'm sure it was devastating from the DePauw standpoint that they just couldn't get the right guys on the field to finish the game. That was an exciting game. We were lucky. We didn't play well for three quarters."

DePauw's Evans could only imagine the outcome if Downham had been able to attempt the thirty-eight-yard field goal. "That was a hell of a way to end it," Evans said. "I certainly had a lot of confidence in the kicker we had. I'll believe for a very long time that we would have made the field goal."

For Curt Selby, the memory of the woeful first half faded away. An incredible comeback completed his first start and, more importantly, his first finish in a Monon Bell Classic. "The old saying 'Wabash Always Fights' was never more true," Selby said. "Even today, if a team gets down and you can hear that chant on the sidelines, it gives me goose bumps. I feel like everybody truly believed it."

Chapter 8

1994: THE ELECTRIC START

WABASH 28, DEPAUW 24

Media attention around the Monon Bell rivalry rose to an all-time high in the mid-1990s. No longer were alums of DePauw and Wabash along with football fans in west central Indiana the only ones paying attention to the tradition-rich rivalry. When the two teams entered the 100th game against each other in 1993 with a dead-even record of 45–45–9, eyes across the country turned to Greencastle and Crawfordsville. National media members wanted to learn more about a rivalry that remained so close and so heated for so long.

National media attention had come before. In 1973, *Sports Illustrated* devoted nine pages and more than six thousand words after writer John Underwood spent time on both campuses the previous year. In 1979, *CBS News Sunday Morning* spent eight minutes featuring the eighty-sixth Monon Bell Classic and brothers Mark (DePauw) and Mike Kepchar (Wabash), who split family allegiances as players on both sides of the rivalry.

Sports Illustrated returned to cover the rivalry in 1993. The 40–26 victory for Wabash was detailed in the November 22 issue that featured a cover story on the Notre Dame–Florida State game in South Bend, Indiana, that pitted the No. 1 and No. 2 teams in Division I against each other. The ND-FSU matchup was labeled by some as the "Game of the Century," but the 100th Monon Bell Classic in Greencastle pitted two teams against each other that had been foes for more than a century. The ten-page ND-FSU spread was followed by a seven-page feature on DePauw-Wabash.

Wabash head coach Greg Carlson made sure to stock a collection of copies of the *Sports Illustrated* story on the 100th game. The national magazine

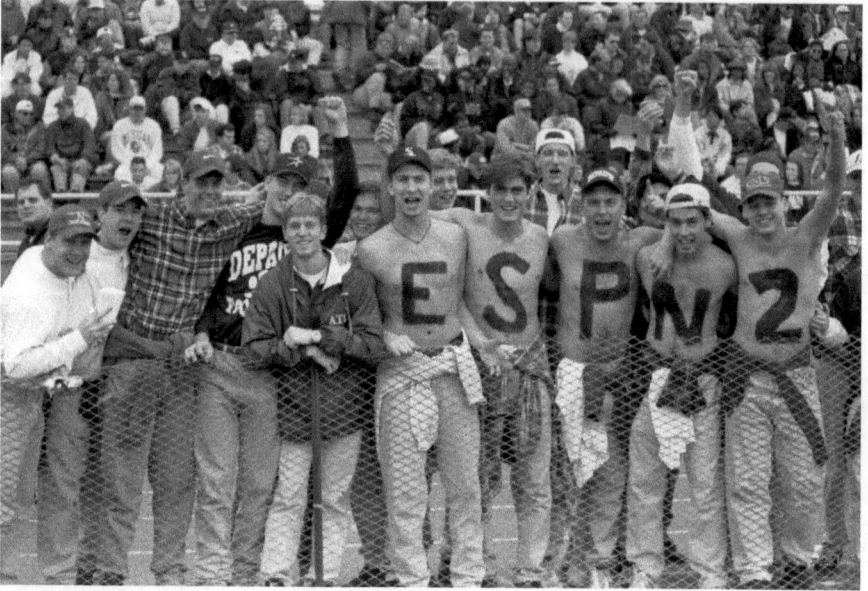

DePauw fans painted themselves with a free advertisement for the network broadcasting the 1994 Monon Bell Classic. *Courtesy of DePauw Archives.*

basically printed additional recruiting material Carlson could use when pitching high school students. "That was unbelievable for recruiting," Carlson said. "I'd go into a high school and throw a *Sports Illustrated* down on the table and say, 'Here's the kind of coverage we're getting from a national media outlet.' That was invaluable for us. I'm sure it was for DePauw even though they lost the game. Just to get recognized by a national sports magazine—that was incredible."

Mike Callahan was a junior linebacker on the losing DePauw squad but still valued the national coverage on small college football programs. "For student-athletes at DePauw and Wabash, that's a big deal," Callahan said. "We're student-athletes that aren't going to play in the NFL. We're not going to have that kinda exposure. It was an exciting time for everyone."

The national attention continued into the 101st game in 1994. ESPN2, only a year old at the time, chose to carry the game on a live national television broadcast. The cameras of "The Worldwide Leader in Sports" would capture the sights of a Division III football game in Crawfordsville. Chris Ings, starting quarterback for the Little Giants, played with plenty of future college football players at Ben Davis High School in Indianapolis, but being featured on ESPN2 brought some bragging rights his way. "It was one of those surreal things. Really, we're on ESPN2? Who would have thought?" Ings said. "I had a fun time giving a hard time to some of my buddies that were playing at least 1-AA football. Check us out. We're on ESPN2, what about you? It was really interesting. Especially with the whole rivalry and how we both had been doing that year and making such a big deal out of it. It was fun."

SECONDS INTO THE 101st Monon Bell Classic, ESPN executives had to be pleased with their decision, as a pair of speedsters for Wabash and DePauw gave the game an unprecedented start for a Monon Bell matchup.

George Lino came to Wabash to run track. Track coach Rob Johnson, with his connections to the United States Track and Field Team, convinced Lino that he could continue a fruitful career in sprinting at Wabash. Recruited out of Arlington High School in Indianapolis, Lino came to Wabash as a five-foot-six, 130-pound freshman and decided to continue his football career while at Wabash as well.

Wabash head football coach Greg Carlson found ways to get the diminutive but blazing Lino on the field as a running back and wide receiver. An ACL injury wiped out what would have been his junior season in 1993, but Lino returned in 1994 feeling as fast as ever. A recorded 4.3-second time in the forty-yard dash helped give him his confidence back. By the time the season finale against DePauw came around, Lino had found ways to put his speed back to good use.

Lino lined up deep as a kick returner awaiting the opening kickoff from DePauw's Pat Evens. The Evens kick carried to the Wabash six-yard line, where Lino corralled the ball near the left hash mark and started up the field. "The thing that stands most vividly in my mind was, as I caught the ball, I still see to this day that wide opening on the left hand side," Lino said. "I remember catching a glimpse of it and making a cut over in that direction."

Lino darted up the field, and by the time he split through the opening at the twenty-five-yard line, he'd already put himself out of reach of most of the DePauw defenders. All he had to do was make a move on Evens. He took an angle farther left toward the DePauw sideline and eluded a diving Evens. By the time he crossed the Wabash forty-yard line, a pair of trailing DePauw Tigers were the only players left for him to outrun. He raised the ball in the direction of the Wabash sideline in celebration after reaching the end zone. Thirteen seconds into the game, Wabash secured a 7–0 lead.

Jon Holloway was not to be outdone. The sophomore defensive back from Indianapolis had running back skills of his own from his prep days at Cathedral High School. By the time he finished his career at DePauw, Holloway set a new school record for career kick-return yardage. The stage awaited him after Lino set the bar high on the opening kick. An Alex Costa kick floated to the five-yard line, where Holloway hauled in the ball on the right side of the field halfway between the hash marks and numbers. Holloway picked up his first block at the twenty-three-yard line and continued down the sidelines, where his blockers set up a running lane. Wabash looked to have him cornered with three would-be-tacklers near the forty-yard line, but Holloway cut sharply toward the middle of the field and left a pile of Little Giants in his dust. "I cut left, and all the other guys kinda just fell over like dominos," Holloway said. "It was like they were on hockey skates. After that it was just run to the end zone."

Holloway crossed midfield and took an angle to the front left corner of the end zone to outrun one last Wabash defender to his right. He flashed the ball in his left hand toward the Wabash sidelines as he finished the final fifteen yards of his ninety-five-yard return. DePauw assistant coach Jeff Voris, who played quarterback for the Tigers in the '80s, was in charge of the kick return unit that day. He felt he couldn't take credit for the outstanding return by Holloway. "We had a kickoff return guy in Jon Holloway who was as good as anyone we were going to play against," Voris said. "He was an outstanding football player."

DePauw and Wabash combined for two touchdowns in the first twenty-nine seconds of the game, but in a bad omen for the Tigers, freshman kicker Jason Gardner failed to convert his extra-point attempt. DePauw trailed 7–6 with fourteen minutes and thirty-one seconds left in the first quarter.

After the game, Holloway's friends asked him what happened to start the game. Their buses from Greencastle hadn't arrived at Wabash in time. "They thought the scoreboard was broken," Holloway said. "They walked in two minutes late and it was already 7–6."

Carlson still hasn't seen a start to a football game that matches the returns of Lino and Holloway. Not a bad way to introduce the ESPN2 audience to the Monon Bell rivalry.

"The opening to that game was the most remarkable opening of a football game I've ever witnessed," Carlson said. "You look up at the scoreboard, and there's fourteen minutes and thirty-one seconds left in the first quarter and it's 7–6. We had ESPN2 there, and I'm pretty sure they're thinking, 'Oh my goodness. We just covered the games of our lives.' So if there's anybody that missed the first several minutes of that game on TV, that's a shame. But if you were watching, you were stuck to that TV the rest of the game. There was no way you weren't watching that game after you saw opening back-to-back kickoff returns for touchdowns."

AFTER THE DUST SETTLED from a blazing start, the game turned over to the hands of Wabash quarterback Chris Ings. The junior from Indianapolis started his third Monon Bell Classic with the expectations as Wabash's next bona fide star. Starting from game one of his freshman year, Ings built an impressive resume with heroic lore following him. In high school, Ings quarterbacked Ben Davis to state championships in his junior and senior seasons. His 1991 senior team earned national championship honors in three major polls.

Ings's collegiate legend, like many others that choose DePauw or Wabash, started when he chose the Little Giants after considering the Tigers for months. In his four years at Wabash, he cemented himself as one of the top recruits that DePauw head coach Nick Mourouzis regretted not being able to land. "I tried to recruit him like mad," Mourouzis said. The confluence of Ings's relationship with Wabash head coach Greg Carlson, a Ben Davis connection to Wabash wide receiver Chris Wiesehan, and the full-ride Lilly Award Scholarship that Wabash presented the quarterback prospect pointed Ings to Crawfordsville.

A cruel introduction to the Monon Bell rivalry greeted Ings as a freshman in 1992. On the first offensive play of the game, Ings threw an interception to the DePauw defense. Ings later helped lead a Wabash comeback while hobbling through a knee injury. Ings thought he'd won the game on a late touchdown pass to Wiesehan, but the play was nullified by a Wabash penalty. With the uncertainty of Ings's health, Carlson decided to settle for a field goal that forced the game to end in a 17–17 tie.

"As a freshman, I was pretty happy," said Ings, who accounted for both Wabash touchdowns with scores on a thirty-two-yard completion to Wiesehan and a one-yard run. "Hey, we got to keep the Monon Bell. Then you look at the seniors that are actually upset about the whole idea of not going for the win."

Ings further redeemed himself the following year with three more touchdown runs in a 40–26 victory. Then, as a junior, he continued to live up to the lofty expectations in the first half of the 1994 tussle when he punctuated two first-quarter touchdown drives with a three-yard run and a thirty-six-yard pass to Pete Logan. A fumbled punt return by Jon Holloway set ups Ings's first touchdown.

In the second quarter, George Lino struck again, this time from the backfield. "The fact that I was smaller...I could kinda get lost in the backfield," Lino said. "It worked out that we had so many good offensive players—a good offensive line—and I was able to sort of capitalize and take advantage because they couldn't see me if I was lining up in the backfield. They were trying to focus on all these other guys. Any one of us at any given time could have an explosive game."

Lino picked the perfect time to have a breakout game. Late in the second quarter, Lino lined up as the lone back behind Ings. After faking right, Lino took a counter handoff from Ings and started left. A free DePauw defender caused Lino to cut back to his right with a defender diving at his heels from behind. The quick moves from Lino put him in the middle of a blocking convoy before he shot past his teammates and nearby defenders. DePauw linebacker Mike Callahan gave chase but could only attempt a hopeless dive at the end of Lino's eighty-four-yard touchdown. "There's nothing like a long touchdown run because it takes so much out of the other team," Lino said. "If someone is on the one-yard line or the two-yard line, there's this anticipation that there's a very good chance that they could score. But the long touchdowns are impactful in that they really take a lot out of the defense."

The Lino touchdown gave Wabash a commanding 28–6 lead that it took into halftime. The Little Giants outgained the Tigers by a 297–94 margin in the first half. Two DePauw fumbles deepened the hole for an inept offensive unit.

PREVIOUS EXPERIENCE TAUGHT GREG CARLSON to anticipate an unexpected momentum shift in a Monon Bell Classic. Eleven seasons as a head coach and three as an assistant at Wabash provided plenty of examples of Little Giant and Tiger comebacks before the 1994 matchup.

"Momentum's always a key factor in any football game, but in a Monon Bell game, because of the crowd, the importance of the game and everything that leads up to the game, you know as a coach that it's not over till it's over. And that's a true statement," Carlson said. "It doesn't matter what the score is going into the fourth quarter or with five minutes left to go in the fourth quarter. You can fumble, they can make a big play, they can intercept a pass and things can turn quickly. As a coach, I don't remember any Monon Bell game where you just said, 'OK, this one's over.' You never really take a breath."

A helpless DePauw defense in the first half forced a momentum shift in the second half, and the previously invincible Chris Ings started to look human.

After DePauw's first offensive series led to another punt, Ings brought the Little Giants out to start a drive near midfield. Then, on second-and-nine, Ings was met by linebacker Tim Cooper blitzing into the backfield to force a fumble. Defensive end Phil Hiscock scooped up the loose ball and rumbled thirty-three yards for a touchdown. This time Jason Gardner converted the extra point to cut Wabash's lead to 28–13.

"We had worked on recovering fumbles all throughout the season and picking it up and running," said Hiscock, crediting assistant coach and former DePauw wide receiver Kevin Perkins with the focus on converting fumbles into returns. "So it occurred very naturally to me. I wasn't really thinking about what I was doing."

Three minutes later, Ings faltered near midfield again. Defensive back Jon Holloway worked all week on a coverage that required him to follow Ings's every move as a spy behind his linebackers. Ings threw the ball over the middle of the field and Holloway stepped in front of the pass and, being no stranger to running in the open field, returned the pick for another defensive touchdown for the Tigers. "He didn't even see me. He was looking over and didn't know that I was lined up right in front of him," Holloway said. "He tried to dink it over the linebackers, and I was just there because I was scouting him. So I ran it back."

The Tiger offense converted a two-point attempt to put the score at 28–21 with nine minutes and seventeen seconds left in the third quarter. A Wabash offense that scored easily in the first half started producing points for DePauw, and suddenly each possession became even more crucial. "We weren't doing what we were supposed to do," said Little Giant running back George Lino. "I was more concerned that we weren't playing up to the level that we should have been playing or that we were capable of playing. It was hard to watch, but internally I was thinking we as a team just have to do a better job."

DePauw quarterback Steve Ganote put together the first offensive scoring threat of the game for the Tigers midway through the third quarter. Passing for thirty-nine yards in the drive, Ganote led the offense to the Wabash eleven-yard line but couldn't muster any more yardage. A twenty-nine-yard Benjamin Fingerhut field goal put another dent in the Wabash lead, but the Tigers remained in a 28–24 hole heading into the fourth quarter.

WHAT STARTED AS A THRILLER turned into a grind-it-out finish. Punts on four straight possessions by the two teams killed the first seven minutes of the fourth quarter. A conservative Wabash offense stopped the streak of turnovers earlier in the second half and worked to run the clock down to hold onto a victory.

A third-and-six at the Wabash twenty-five presented a key moment in the game. A stop, and DePauw's offense would have plenty of time to find a way to score a touchdown. A first down, and Wabash would continue to drain the time on the clock. Chris Ings dropped back to pass, but defensive end Mike Callahan made his way into the backfield and dragged the star quarterback down. Trying to wrestle down the elusive Ings, Callahan grabbed a hold of him with one hand in front and one hand on the back of his shoulder pads. The sack for an eight-yard loss would have forced Wabash to punt. Instead, Callahan was flagged for a fifteen-yard facemask penalty. The tackle forced Ings's head down, but video replays didn't show a clear violation by Callahan. A picture from the play now hangs in the bedroom of Callahan's son. He doesn't remember grabbing any of Ings's facemask. The ESPN2 footage would be available for the DePauw players to watch and wonder what could have been.

"I remember looking at it and Callahan being very upset over that particular play just because he knew that Ings was faking it when he gestured to the ref that his facemask was pulled," said defensive lineman Phil Hiscock. "It was definitely very upsetting for him and for all of us, especially after watching it after the fact."

"At the time, it was a tough pill to swallow," Callahan said. "It was certainly something that I thought about for a long time after the fact."

Wabash ran the clock down to under four minutes, but DePauw's offense received one last chance. Quarterback Steve Ganote moved DePauw's offense to as far as its own forty-eight-yard line, but the drive ended without points for the eleventh time in the game. Ryan Pitcock sealed the game for Wabash with an interception with barely a minute left in the game.

The twenty-eight first-half points for Wabash proved to be enough for Little Giants victory number forty-seven in the rivalry. The mistakes in the second half lingered with Ings, but for the third year in a row with him at the helm, the Monon Bell remained on the Wabash campus for another year. He completed an undefeated career against DePauw the following year.

"We just didn't play well offensively," Ings said. "We were just making mistake after mistake. We were a great offensive football team that year. We had some untimely struggles, and they had some big plays. It came down right to the wire. We were fortunate to win that one."

Chapter 9

2001: THE TIP TO THE CATCH

WABASH 27, DEPAUW 21

Wabash College needed a change. Greg Carlson won 112 games as the head coach of the Little Giants football team, but his success against rival DePauw had waned. After losing to the Tigers for five straight years, Carlson was let go despite a .661 winning percentage in eighteen seasons at the head of the program. Only Pete Vaughan, who coached at Wabash from 1919 to 1945, won more football games (113) for the small college in Crawfordsville.

To replace Carlson, who had compiled a 7–10–1 record against DePauw, Wabash turned to a coach familiar with small college football in the Midwest. Chris Creighton, then head coach at Ottawa University in Kansas, led Kenyon (Ohio) College to a conference championship in 1989 as a quarterback during a career that ended with all-American honors. In 1999, Wabash joined Kenyon in the same conference Creighton won—the North Coast Athletic Conference—and the Little Giant football program completed its first season in the conference in 2000.

Creighton was charged with leading the Little Giants to the top of the new conference and bringing back the Monon Bell to Wabash's campus. Players like junior linebacker Nate Boulais felt the difference that Creighton brought to the program immediately. "Part of the reason why Coach Creighton was attractive to us was because we wanted something bigger," Boulais said. "We wanted more out of the program. He was a guy that was certainly going to push us that way."

Creighton set the new standard in the spring semester of 2001. He started to weed out players less dedicated to winning with fourteen weeks of 6:00

a.m. player workouts. Grueling early morning workouts put an emphasis on discipline for students already being challenged academically at the same time. The program lost twenty to thirty players by the time the semester ended, but the fifty-plus that remained all shared the same goals heading into the summer.

Ryan Short was coached by Creighton only for his last two years at Wabash, but the new coach left a lasting impression. From the moment Creighton took over the program, Short felt a new standard not only for Wabash but also for the entire coaching profession. "I've always compared the greatest coaches that I've met to him ever since then. He's just a whole-different-level type of guy. You realize that when you meet him," Short said. "He created a different level of excitement for the program. I thought there was already a lot, but he brought even more energy and excitement to the program."

By the time the fall rolled around, Creighton led Wabash to a 7–2 record heading into the annual season finale with DePauw. His team rebounded from consecutive losses to Wheaton and Wittenberg in September with six straight victories. Creighton then had to learn what to expect from the Monon Bell rivalry. "They tried to prepare me for it, and I thought it sounded a little over the top," Creighton said. "I'll never forget when [Wabash Director of Sports Information] Brent Harris sat me down and said how many media requests he had for the week. It was obviously a really big deal, but then it surpassed whatever expectations I would have had in that first year."

Creighton might not have known what to expect, but his players certainly did. Boulais came to Wabash in the fall of 1999 in the midst of the Monon Bell drought. "Every professor I had for class, every dean I met on campus, every older guy in the Phi Delt house at Wabash said, 'Hey, how are we looking this year?' The second question would be 'Are we going to win the Bell?' You realized how much it meant to the school. It's like winning the Super Bowl. You learn really quickly how important it was to everybody."

The Wabash seniors had yet to ring the Monon Bell in their three previous seasons. No player on the roster had tasted victory over its archrivals. The motivation to win couldn't have been higher. That's why Creighton decided not to throw any more pressure on his players. He trusted that they could be self-motivated. "I think the rivalry got so cranked up that guys weren't relaxed when they played," Creighton said. "I came in with the approach that it's not just any other game—obviously that's not the case. We just wanted them to be in the moment and to play." Creighton had only one motto for his team. "Our theme for the year was 'We Believe.' As a coach,

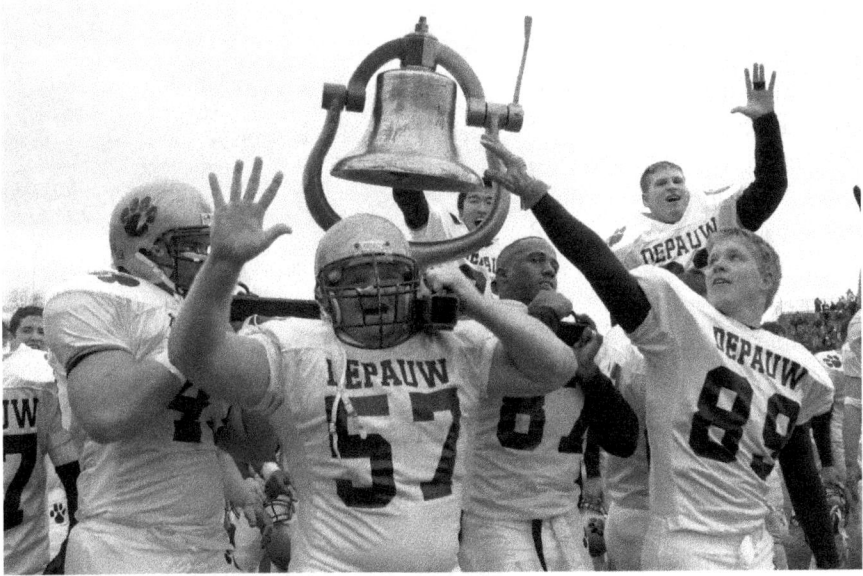

The DePauw Tigers won their fifth straight Monon Bell Classic in 2000 with a 27–17 score. *Courtesy of DePauw Archives.*

when you live your theme, you have a special year," said Creighton. "We always spend a lot of time thinking about what the program needs to do to be its best. That first year at Wabash, it was 'We Believe.'"

As the final seconds ticked away in the 2001 Monon Bell Classic, Wabash's theme couldn't be more fitting.

A VICTORIOUS DEPAUW TEAM kept five fingers in the air while celebrating with the Monon Bell in 2000. Since the first game between the two schools in 1890, DePauw had beaten Wabash five straight times only once before. The streak spanning 1996 to 2000 matched a streak of the same length from 1960 to 1964. In the five straight wins, DePauw held a 135–51 scoring advantage with only one game decided by fewer than 10 points. DePauw displayed a talent gap between the two schools at times, but good fortune and grittiness played a role in the streak as well.

In 2000, Ryan Short thought his Wabash team was the better of the two. Instead, DePauw went into Crawfordsville and pulled out a 27–17 comeback victory to take an overall series lead of 50–48–9. Wabash led 17–9 after Short caught an eleven-yard touchdown pass from Jake Knott with nine minutes and fifty-five seconds left in the fourth quarter, but DePauw surged ahead with the play of quarterback Jason Lee and wide receiver John Stephens, despite their injured body parts. The two connected for a thirty-yard touchdown to cut the deficit to 17–15 before a fifteen-yard Jackson Rust touchdown run gave the Tigers a 21–17 lead with minutes and six seconds left in the game. A twenty-five-yard touchdown pass from Lee to Stephens iced the game with slightly more than a minute left. Stephens, the receiver, played with a broken wrist, and Lee, the quarterback, played on a torn ACL in his left leg.

Lee hurt his knee in the eighth game of the season against Centre College and sat out the ninth game against Rose-Hulman Institute of Technology. He found a way to hold himself together for the final game of his junior season. "The doctor said you

DePauw quarterback Jason Lee led the Tigers to a 27–17 win in the 2000 Monon Bell Classic despite playing with a torn ACL in his left leg. The victory marked the fifth straight for DePauw. *Courtesy of DePauw Archives.*

can't really do anything worse to it, so it was kinda taped in a position where it wouldn't bend, and I had a big brace," Lee said. "I wasn't that mobile to begin with, so the offensive line knew they had a challenge."

Not yet having had a chance to play in a Monon Bell game, Lee was willing to play through the pain in order to put his mark on the rivalry that helped sway him to come to DePauw from North Central High School in Indianapolis. "You get that opportunity to play in one of these big games where it's kinda bigger than yourself," Lee said. "You get to watch all these other major college football teams steeped in tradition on Saturdays, and its fun to be a part of one of those types of games. That was one of the reasons I went to DePauw originally, and I was going to do everything to play in as many of those games as I could."

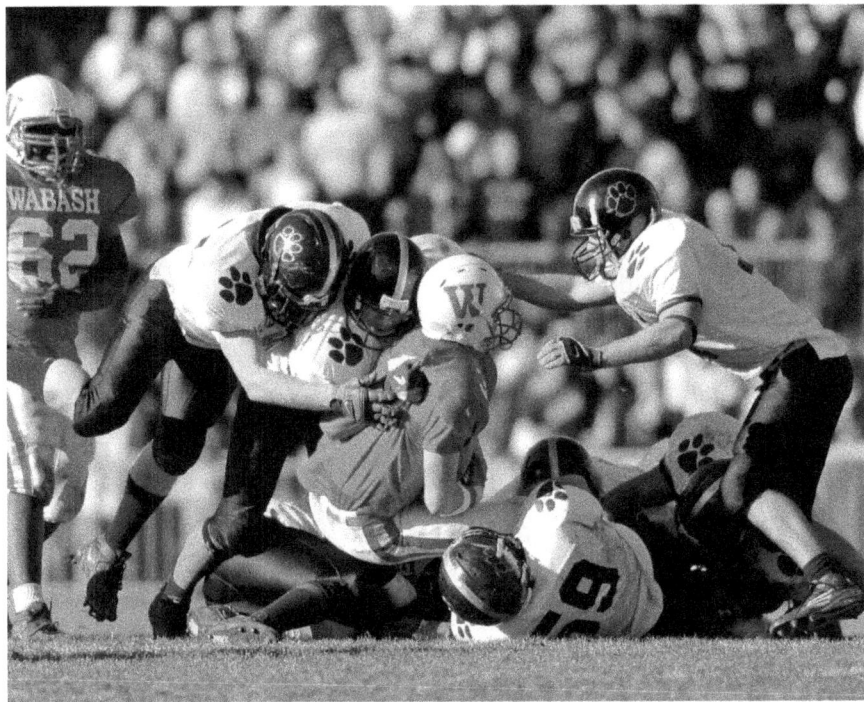

An ambush of DePauw Tigers tackles a Wabash ball carrier. *Courtesy of DePauw Archives.*

As a senior, and with two healthy legs, Lee would get a chance to extend DePauw's winning streak against Wabash to a program-record six games.

CHRIS CREIGHTON WANTED TO BRING some civility to the game. He'd heard stories of fights before, both during and after Monon Bell games. Following multiple altercations between the teams and their fans following games in the '90s, the two schools decided to have the Bell moved to a neutral end zone in the fourth quarter. Previously, if a team lost the Bell, it had to face the opposing team rushing to its sideline to reclaim the trophy. Naturally some shoves and words were exchanged. Placing the Bell in an end zone prevented the teams from crossing paths after the game.

Creighton wanted to take the sportsmanship a step further. On Tuesday before the 2001 game, the athletic directors and head coaches of both schools met for a lunch. That's where Creighton learned that a postgame handshake between teams had been absent from recent traditions. "I basically said, 'Look, my mom will send me to my room if my football team doesn't shake hands after the game. We're shaking hands after the game.' To his credit, [Mourouzis] agreed."

The plan sounded good, but Creighton had yet to be truly introduced to the atmosphere of a Monon Bell game. There was a reason Jake Knott, junior quarterback on the 2001 team and son of former Wabash quarterback Dave Knott, went to a number of Wabash football games growing up but wasn't allowed to attend a Monon Bell game. He didn't get to experience his first game atmosphere until he started his freshman year. Creighton's first taste came that Saturday. "We're driving the bus into the parking lot, and there were people throwing stuff at the bus and giving you the bird," Creighton said. "The student section is there chanting vulgarities an hour and a half before the game as your guys are warming up. We're just looking at each other smiling like, 'You gotta be kidding me,' but in a cool way."

Maybe a simple postgame handshake line would be harder than he thought.

THE GAME COULDN'T HAVE STARTED much better for Wabash. DePauw's offense started the game's first possession but four plays into the opening drive gave the ball to Wabash courtesy of a fumble by running back Matt King and a recovery by Dustin Deno. That's when Jake Knott put in motion an offense that moved the ball down the field against DePauw one series after another in the first half. Wabash's first drive ended with a three-yard touchdown pass from Knott to Nick Dawson, and Wabash grabbed an early 7–0 lead with nine minutes and seven seconds left in the first quarter.

The next three Wabash drives took the Little Giants inside DePauw's 10-yard line. But four drives of 177 yards resulted in just a 14–0 lead. The second drive stalled with two Wabash penalties for a loss of 25 yards after reaching the DePauw 7-yard line and ended with a punt. Another DePauw fumble led to a 15-yard touchdown pass from Knott to junior tight end Ryan Short, ending the third drive of the game for the Little Giants. The fourth drive ended on DePauw's 1-yard line when Val Benoit was denied on a fourth-and-goal by the Tiger defense.

The fifth drive started at the DePauw twenty-two and ended four plays later with a turnover on downs. The Wabash offense left points on the board while its defense stifled the Tiger offense for nearly two quarters. DePauw's offense found life only after Wabash's Stu Johnson fumbled a punt return and gave the Tigers the ball on the twenty-yard line. A Jason Lee pass to Dan Ryan for a four-yard touchdown gave DePauw its first glimmer of hope with two minutes left in the first half. Despite a statistical onslaught, Wabash led by only seven points at halftime.

Wabash redeemed a lost lead in the 2000 Monon Bell Classic with a last-second victory in the 2001 matchup at DePauw's Blackstock Stadium. *Courtesy of DePauw Archives.*

A third quarter full of punts and turnovers kept the score the same until DePauw tied the game with one minute and forty seconds left in the quarter. A forty-eight-yard completion from Lee to Mark Rinehart set up a three-yard touchdown run for King. Wabash was unable to regain control of the game until DePauw fumbled the ball for the fourth time. Wide receiver John Stephens let the ball loose and gave Wabash the ball at its own forty-yard line.

Knott was ready to put his mark on the game. A two-yard run on fourth-and-one at the Wabash forty-nine-yard line kept the drive alive. On the very next play, Knott threw to Josh Bronaugh for a forty-eight-yard completion. Following a five-yard penalty on first down, Knott connected with Short again for a six-yard touchdown pass, and the Little Giants took a 21–14 lead with ten minutes and fourteen seconds left in the game.

Having lost a late lead the previous season, cautious excitement filled the Wabash sideline. Each play ticked away the seconds standing between Wabash and its first Bell victory since 1995. DePauw's ensuing drive ended with three incomplete passes at the Wabash twenty-five. Knott then gave the ball back to DePauw with an interception, but DePauw failed to convert the turnover into points after driving into the red zone. Now four minutes and forty-three seconds remained, and Knott needed to open up a larger lead to seal the game. The drive halted when three straight running plays led to another Wabash punt and gave the ball back to DePauw with one minute and twenty-two seconds remaining.

The game would still need punctuation from Knott in the final minute.

RYAN SHORT SAW HIS TEAM fall apart in the fourth quarter one too many times. All of a sudden, he was having flashbacks to the 2000 loss, fearing that he and his fellow offensive teammates had not scored enough points to give the defense a comfortable lead. He could only watch as DePauw moved down the field in the final minute. "It really reminded me of my sophomore year because they just started plugging away. And in a football game, you kinda loosen up your defense and tighten up your offense, and it's the perfect recipe for a comeback."

A short sixteen-yard punt out of bounds by Wabash's Joe Lonnemann left DePauw sixty-one yards away from tying the game with a touchdown and an extra point. For one last time, quarterback Jason Lee hoped to lead his team to victory. He'd need to orchestrate a no-huddle offense with no timeouts, guide his team into the end zone and force the first overtime in Monon Bell history in order to have the chance.

After an incompletion on first down, Lee completed a pass to running back Matt King for sixteen yards to cross midfield. Another first-down incompletion brought the clock to fifty-nine seconds. Then King connected with wide receiver John Stephens for twenty-two yards to the twenty-three-yard line. Three plays later, Lee found King again for a seventeen-yard reception to the six-yard line.

Standing in the shotgun, Lee took the first-and-goal snap with the clock running and thirty-four seconds remaining. Throwing from the fifteen-yard line, Lee found Stephens cutting across the middle of the field. Stephens caught the pass at the six and headed to the goal line, where he was greeted by a trio of Wabash defenders who tackled him at the one.

As the referees stopped the clock to set the ball and down marker, DePauw offensive coordinator Matt Walker sent a jumbo offensive package into the game. It was a decision he immediately regretted. With less than twenty seconds left and no timeouts, an unsuccessful running play would have left the offense scrambling on third down with few receiving options on the field. "If we get stuffed here, we have time to get off another play, but we clearly couldn't run it again," Walker said. "I'd have to run all these skill guys back on and get back in a throw look. I'm like, 'This is really dumb.' I'm almost ready to throw up because I feel so bad about having done what I just did."

Matt Walker directs DePauw in his third Monon Bell Classic as a head coach in 2008. Walker worked six years as an assistant coach for DePauw and played for the Tigers from 1997 to 1999. The Tigers won seven of the thirteen Monon Bell games during Walker's years with the program. *Courtesy of Alex Turco.*

Walker's players bailed him out. Lee took the snap with just under seventeen seconds and handed the ball left to King, who followed the push of his offensive line to fall into the end zone. An extra point tied the game with fourteen seconds left in the fourth quarter. "We scored and tied the game, but really it was a big screw-up," Walker said. "We should have just been throwing it, or at least if we were going to run it, we needed to keep our throw package out there and we didn't. Thank God we scored."

If DePauw was thanking God, then Wabash would be praying to Mary moments later. Each second was precious.

DePauw hoped a squib kick would force a frazzled Wabash team to waste time on the kickoff, but freshman Eddie Garza fielded the ball cleanly and went down at the Wabash thirty-seven-yard line, using only 4 seconds. The Little Giants called a timeout with 10 seconds left in regulation and set up a quick pass to senior wide receiver Kurt Casper, who entered the game leading the team in receiving yards but had been limited to just two catches for thirty yards heading into the final drive. On first down, Knott rifled the ball to Casper, who was hit immediately by DePauw defender Cory Partlow, for a nine-yard gain. As Casper went to the ground, he immediately called for a timeout with 2.7 seconds left on the clock. "He was really our last option," Knott said of Casper. "He got absolutely hammered. As he's getting killed, he's calling timeout. It's two plays right in a row where guys were coached well. They were prepared, and they did exactly what they needed to do in that situation—one by a freshman and another by one of our team leaders and captains that year, Kurt, who had given a lot to the program and was just battling his ass off to find a way to go out on top."

Knott and Casper headed to the sideline to decide on one final play in regulation with Creighton. Casper wanted a hook-and-ladder. Creighton waffled between that and their special version of a Hail Mary. Knott wanted the long heave. Knott's voice won out. The play: Colorado Red, an homage to the sixty-four-yard, game-winning Hail Mary pass Colorado's Kordell Stewart threw to Michael Westbrook to beat Michigan with no time left on September 24, 1994.

The play's concept was simple, but the execution was complicated. Knot recalled:

> *We practiced it every Friday. We knew exactly what we wanted to do in that situation. We had never used it—we had never been in that situation to use it—but it's like any other play. You practice a lot of things in football that you just don't know when you're going to need it, like a four-minute drill trying to make sure you wind the clock all the way down to a second every play or*

when you need to run one play and then run the field goal team on in less than sixteen seconds. There are all these situations that you practice; you just don't use them lot of the time. But you gotta be prepared to use them.

Three wide receivers lined up on one side of the field and sprint for the end zone. Knott aimed for Ryan Short, a six-foot-five target. Depending on where Short was able to get to the ball, Kurt Casper would tell him what to do. "It didn't work very often in practice because it was so complex," Casper said. "The way the play worked was that if Ryan Short, who was the tight end at the time, was in the end zone, I would either tell him to catch it or tip it. If he were short of the end zone, he would tip it. In most cases, less than 50 percent of the time, it didn't work against air."

Short learned in practice just how hard intentionally tipping a football could be. The oblong shape of a football doesn't lend itself to a normal bounce. "I would practice tipping it, and we had about a 40 or 50 percent success rate in practice," Short said. "It's not a volleyball. Tipping a football is a very difficult process. There was a little bit of luck as much as I try not to admit it."

On the sidelines, Creighton challenged his team to live the theme he gave the team earlier in the season: "We Believe." He started chanting the two words, and his players followed. With a plan and a prayer, Knott took the snap with 2.7 seconds remaining on the clock. He rolled to his right, where three Wabash receivers departed downfield on the snap of the ball. DePauw, in a prevent defense, sent most of its secondary back deep to protect the goal line but also sent two defenders to jam Wabash receivers at the line of scrimmage. Linebacker Jason Geringer matched up against Wabash's Nick Dawson, and defensive back Obinna Ugokwe tried to knock Kurt Casper off his route. Lined up in between those two receivers, tight end Ryan Short was able to get off the line free and head for the end zone unmolested.

Waiting near the end zone, DePauw defensive back David Blackburn spied Short nearing the goal line and sized him up. The five-foot-nine defensive back would have to time his jump perfectly to deny the much taller Short. Back near midfield, Knott rolled to his right near the Wabash sideline eyeing his target. While Knott was giving his receivers time to get to the end zone, DePauw defensive lineman JT Benton started to close in on Knott. The quarterback approached the line of scrimmage and launched the ball downfield just before Benton crushed him onto the sideline.

The trajectory of Knott's throw carried the ball to near the five-yard line. Short, waiting by the goal line, drifted forward hoping to out-leap the black jerseys surrounding him. Blackburn jumped in front of Short and linebacker

Mike Laszynski lunged behind the Wabash receiver. Two more DePauw defenders—John Christophersen and Freddy Marrero—were stuck a couple yards behind Short's back unable to make a play on the ball. "The ball was in the air, and I saw it," Blackburn said. "I was in front of the ball, and I tried to come toward it and jump up and knock it down. I just wasn't tall enough to climb that ladder."

Short reached higher than his surrounding defenders to deflect the ball toward the end zone, where Kurt Casper waited one yard across the goal line. The ball bounced directly toward Casper, who quickly jumped to catch the ball and win the game for Wabash. He turned directly to the Wabash crowd and raised his arms in jubilance before Dawson and Short took him to the ground.

"I looked back, and it just fell in his hands," Blackburn said. "It was just like, 'Oh my God. You gotta be kidding.' It was kinda like slow motion. There was no way it just landed in his hands like that."

Back near midfield, Knott couldn't see a thing. Benton's hit knocked him under a bench on the Wabash sideline. Then he heard the eruption.

A dog pile of Wabash players formed on top of Casper near the end zone, and the DePauw defenders were left to escape the celebration of the players and fans rushing onto the field. In the midst of the madness, Geringer grabbed the ball Casper dropped during the celebration and headed back toward the DePauw sideline. He punted the ball in frustration and unbuttoned his chinstrap.

Back on the DePauw sideline, the home team stood stunned. Players buckled, overcome by the emotion of a game lost on the final play. DePauw head coach Nick Mourouzis couldn't believe what he witnessed. "You figured, 'We stop them here, and we go into overtime,'" Mourouzis said. "We had momentum, and they knew it, too. To lose that way, you go from a high all the way down. That's the lowest I've ever felt. I've never gone through such an extreme change in emotion in such a short time."

Matt Walker didn't even see the play. He had his back turned to the field while planning the offensive strategy for overtime. When he heard the Wabash crowd, he experienced "a feeling I've never had before." "I couldn't believe it. I've never had a change in emotion quicker than that in my life," Walker said.

With the Bell waiting to be taken back to Crawfordsville, the celebration was halted as both teams formed a handshake line from sideline to sideline. In the face of defeat, DePauw managed to hold its end of the deal on the agreement Wabash head coach Chris Creighton advocated for earlier that week.

"There was a sea of people flooding the place, but our guys went to shake their hands, and their guys came to shake our hands," Creighton said. "The credit goes to DePauw and to their character because that would have been the most difficult moment to change the tide on shaking hands. And they did that. Then our guys went and got the Bell. To me, that's how it needs to be. Credit DePauw for making that happen."

THE QUESTION STILL REMAINS: how exactly did the ball travel from Ryan Short at the five-yard line to Kurt Casper waiting in the end zone. Casper and quarterback Jake Knott were the first to bust Short's chops and joke that the ball bounced off his helmet. The same sentiment still exists for some on the losing team that day.

"A lot of people say that it was a tipped pass back to the receiver," said DePauw linebacker Jason Geringer, who saw the play unfold from where he was guarding Mike Dawson nearby. "I still swear through and through that the ball bounced off his helmet and he missed it. I don't think it was actually tipped. I think he tried to tip it...but I swear it hit off his helmet and bounced back into the end zone." After the game, Nick Mourouzis's son, Ted, told his dad the same thing. "He goes up, he misses it and it hits him," Mourouzis said. "How do you lose like that?

Short has pored over the film of that play like a conspiracy theorist looking for evidence of John F. Kennedy's shooter on the grassy knoll. The footage shows Casper reaching with both hands above his head like a volleyball setter as the ball approaches. When the ball flies toward Casper, Short's hands then separate to the side. It's unclear whether Casper's helmet or hands played a large role in the deflection. To Short, the answer is physics. "If it hit my helmet, it would have bounced a lot differently," Short said. Instead, Short said he used his hands to guide the ball toward Casper. The momentum of the throw took care of the rest.

So the what-ifs live on. What if JT Benton had tracked down Casper a second sooner instead of hitting him after the ball was released? What if the game had gone to overtime? As Knott remembers it, he's not sure he would have been able to play in overtime after the hit he took from Benton. "I didn't break my hand, but it would have been pretty difficult for me to play in overtime," Knott said. "You don't know because maybe adrenaline takes over and you figure it out, but I couldn't really shake hands after the game or that night."

What if Wabash's defense didn't surrender the lead to DePauw with less than a minute left in the first place?

"I couldn't enjoy the win," said Wabash linebacker Nate Boulais. "I was so disgusted that we gave up a touchdown with under two minutes to go. I

The Monon Bell, circa 2004. *Courtesy of DePauw Archives.*

was praying that we went to overtime. I wanted to win in overtime so that we'd win defensively."

One what-if that didn't happen prevails over all: What if Wabash didn't believe?

"We Believe" started as a cliché motto that sounded perfectly crafted for team T-shirts. Then it became the lasting legacy of the 2001 Wabash Little Giants.

"Coach Creighton had talked about this exact type of scenario," Boulais said. "There's going to be some kind of scenario where you feel like there's no possible way to win, and we'll figure out a way to win."

When that moment confronted Wabash, the Little Giants lived up to Creighton's promise.

"The moment wasn't the catch," Creighton said. "It was, 'Do we believe when there's only ten seconds left and all the momentum has just shifted and their crowd is going crazy and our crowd is quiet?' That's when I remember going up and down the sidelines basically challenging our guys, just saying, 'Did we think it was going to be easy? Do we believe or not?' And then obviously our guys responded. It was just complete euphoria."

Chapter 10

2007: THE KICK FROM THE QUESTION MARK

DEPAUW 24, WABASH 21

W ho is Jordan Havercamp?

That was the question DePauw's student-run TV station asked in an accidentally prescient segment for its 2007 Monon Bell pregame coverage. A reporter spent time with Havercamp, and the two poked fun at his lack of playing time and relative anonymity on the football team. As part of a mocking interview, the reporter asked the sophomore reserve kicker, "What's your philosophy during practice?" Havercamp responded with, "Well, you know, coaches always say you should practice like you play, and well, I don't really play much, so I don't feel like I should take any kicks in practice because I don't kick in the game."

Part of that was true. Havercamp hadn't attempted any field goals in the first nine games of the 2007 season for DePauw, his first with the team after transferring from Denison in the winter of his freshman year. But he had kicked plenty in practice, even as the coaching staff questioned his dedication to the team. That season provided Havercamp with a heavy dose of reality. When he transferred from Denison, he was so confident in his kicking ability that he didn't even reach out to the DePauw coaches beforehand. "[Whether it was] arrogance or not, I figured I would just walk on to another D-3 field and take the spot," Havercamp said. "I didn't really care what the situation was there. I just figured that would be the case."

Havercamp didn't bring much of a resume with him from Denison. As a freshman in 2006, he missed his lone field goal attempt of the season, hit both of his extra point attempts and spent most of his time as a kickoff specialist with a 52.6-yard average on thirty-six kicks. He saw action in the first game of the season for DePauw, but it came with two minutes and seven seconds left in a 47–7 blowout win over Anderson University. Havercamp knocked through the final extra point of the game and booted the ensuing kickoff.

The season opener was a distant memory by the eve of the Monon Bell game. That's when Havercamp once again saw Brendan Smith slated above him as the starting kicker on the pregame depth chart. The end of a frustrating season was nearing. "I was furious," Havercamp said. "I was thinking I went the entire season and didn't get a start. The reason I went to this school was so I wouldn't get redshirted. I had basically been redshirted because of this. I was ticked off."

In the locker room, Havercamp started venting to sophomore offensive lineman David Joeckel. The backup kicker even considered not showing up for the next day's game, but his teammate and Sigma Chi fraternity brother talked him out of it.

Less than twenty-four hours later, Joeckel wouldn't be the only one glad Havercamp showed up.

CHRIS CREIGHTON HAD WABASH ROLLING. The Little Giants entered the 2007 Monon Bell Classic with a 9–0 record and were looking for the fourth perfect regular season in school history. Wabash found success in the North Coast Athletic Conference with four conference titles in Creighton's seven years but also strung together an impressive streak against rival DePauw. The Little Giants won two Monon Bell games in a row and five of the last six spanning back to the last-second victory in 2001.

Confidence came in bunches with the 2007 Wabash team. In preparation for the game, the team may have already had its eyes on the Division III playoffs. "We had no doubt we were going to win the game," said starting quarterback Matt Hudson. "When we watched them on film, we knew they were a good team at 7–2 coming in out of a tough conference. We were undefeated at the time, and we were almost like this is a formality. Let's just finish off this perfect regular season and go into the playoffs with hopefully a No. 1 seed and a lot of momentum."

A sophomore, Hudson wasn't supposed to be leading this team into the Monon Bell game. Fifth-year senior Dustin Huff, a preseason all-American, led the Little Giants into the season but broke his leg in the closing seconds of a 35–33 win over Franklin College. Huff threw for 477 yards and four touchdowns in the victory but suffered the injury as a member of the hands team trying to recover an onside kick by Franklin.

Wabash fans cheer on their team during the 2007 Monon Bell Classic at DePauw's Blackstock Stadium. *Courtesy of Alex Turco.*

After sophomore transfer Kyle Augustinovicz was given a chance to start the next two games of the season, Hudson took hold of the quarterback position in the second half of game three at Ohio Wesleyan University. Hudson entered a scoreless tie and threw for two touchdowns in a 15–0 win. By the time the regular season finale rolled around, Hudson had thrown for 1,710 yards and seventeen touchdowns.

Hudson's first experience with the rivalry came back in 2005, when he sat in the Blackstock Stadium bleachers as a DePauw recruit and watched the Little Giants win back the Bell. Now he was set to return to Blackstock and start his own legacy in the rivalry.

A defensive first quarter developed in front of eight thousand fans to start the 114th matchup between Wabash and DePauw. The pace favored the Tigers, whose time-crunching running attack led by Jeremiah Marks had defined the team throughout the season. The DePauw defense managed to hold a Little Giants offense, one averaging 35.7 points per game with Hudson as the starter, scoreless for fifteen minutes. But the last play of the quarter offered a glimpse of the high-powered offense Hudson steered throughout the season. He hit senior wide receiver Mike Russell for a 49-yard completion and put the Wabash offense on DePauw's 6-yard line. Three plays later, Hudson gave Wabash the first lead of the game on a 1-yard quarterback sneak. A Drew Oehler kick made the score 7–0 Little Giants.

The Tigers responded on the next drive with the legs of Marks and the hands of Bryan Mulligan. A poor kickoff from Oehler gave DePauw the ball at the Wabash forty-six-yard line, an opportunity the Tigers wouldn't waste. In eight plays, including six Marks rushing attempts for thirty-one yards, the Tigers tie the game. Mulligan, a sophomore receiver, caught a ten-yard touchdown for the first DePauw score on its second trip into the red zone on the day. Kicker Brendan Smith missed a twenty-five-yard field goal attempt to end the first red-zone trip, so Jordan Havercamp came on to nail the ensuing extra point for a 7–7 tie.

The big-play Wabash offense took little time to regain the lead. The following drive was highlighted by an eighteen-yard Hudson run and a thirty-eight-yard pass to Russell before C.P. Porter crossed the goal line on a two-yard rush. An offensive onslaught appeared to be underway at Blackstock with Wabash leading 14–7.

DePauw continued to have success moving the ball as well. A deficit didn't change the Tiger game plan, and Marks and Mulligan were well on their way to record-setting days. Twelve consecutive plays ended with the ball in the hands of one of the two players, and the Tigers marched sixty-three yards down to the two-yard line. Sophomore quarterback Spud Dick mixed in short passes with the repetitive running game.

With just twenty-eight seconds left in the half, head coach Matt Walker called timeout with a third-and-goal play awaiting his offensive unit. Marks had been stuffed on the two previous goal-line plays, so he decided on a different strategy. On third down, Dick faked a handoff right to Marks and looked into the right flat, where senior fullback Brett Claxton found an opening. Dick's pass floated past a jumping Little Giant defensive end and landed in Claxton's hands one yard from the goal line. The only things separating the five-foot-ten, 235-pound Claxton from the end zone were the white-painted "G" signifying the goal line and all-American linebacker Adi Pynenberg. The five-foot-eleven, 213-pound defender stoned the opposing fullback, and Claxton fell backward before the football could cross the plane into the end zone.

Pynenberg entered the game with 407 tackles in his career, a school record, but none were bigger at that point. The Wabash defense needed one more play to complete the stand. Walker elected to attempt another pass on fourth down, but Dick's throw fell incomplete with eleven seconds left in the

A group of Wabash defenders knock DePauw wide receiver Bryan Mulligan out of bounds during the 2007 Monon Bell Classic. Mulligan set a Monon Bell record for catches in a game with fifteen receptions for 145 yards. *Courtesy of Alex Turco.*

half. Hudson ran a sneak from his own goal line, and the visitors took a 14–7 lead into the locker room.

"I can remember being really mad at myself on that one," Walker said. "We had Jeremiah Marks, who was arguably one of the top two or three short-yardage backs in the nation at that point. We should have just handed it to him four times, and he would have freakin' scored on one of them. We got fancy. We threw it to Claxton once in the flat, and he got blasted. We tried play-action to the tight end and it gets knocked down. It was stupid by me."

Walker would have to figure out a way to redeem himself in the second half if DePauw was going to win.

THE WEIGHT OF A MONON BELL MATCHUP had long been understood by Matt Walker. It was a tradition passed down by his father, Dick, who graduated from DePauw in 1968, and his proximity to Wabash while growing up in Crawfordsville. He'd seen countless clashes between the two in-state rivals, and when it was his turn to make a college decision, he followed the path of his father.

DePauw won all three games against Wabash with Walker on the team as a quarterback from 1996 to 1998. He took the final snap in a 42–7 victory in his senior year and still hasn't lost possession of that ball after having his brother stash it away following the game. So when Walker was named DePauw's head coach in 2006 after six seasons as an assistant, he knew how to approach the annual classic—at least how he thought it should be approached:

> *I probably treated it a lot different than many of the coaches from Wabash or DePauw in that I didn't ever try to treat it like just another game, because it wasn't. As much as you may want to think that that was the right way to handle it, I knew from playing in it and being an assistant coach in it that it was different because you didn't even feel the same. Your body felt different. You almost felt like you were out of your body that day for a while. I remember that first year, I told myself, "I'm going to go against what a lot of people probably think the right way is to handle this." I firmly believe that no matter what you tell them [the players]—how you try to trick them or what not—they weren't going to feel the same that day. From the second you stepped off the bus that day, it was so different. Warm-ups were different…there was such a different buzz and feel. Why am I going to sit here and try to spin to the guys that we're going to treat this like any other game?*

Instead, Walker tried to channel the emotion and energy that takes over both campuses the week of the Monon Bell game for something meaningful. His team suffered a 23–20 loss at Wabash in his first year as head coach, but a home environment at Blackstock Stadium offered something different.

"I'm going to agree with you that this is going to be different. I'm not going to treat it the same. But I'm only going to do that if we agree that we're going to use what makes it different to practice that much harder, to study film that much harder, to work that much harder," Walker said. "You're going to feel different during the week. You're going to feel different when you go to the weight room. That's fine. Let's agree that that's going to be the case, but let's make sure that the different thing—whatever it is that's hard to define, let's make sure it feeds into something that makes us…work harder and be more intense."

INTENSITY WAS NEVER A PROBLEM for Jeremiah Marks. By the time the last game of his college football career came against Wabash, Marks had

DePauw running back Jeremiah Marks rushed for 181 yards and caught seven passes for 97 yards and two touchdowns in a winning effort during the 2007 Monon Bell Classic. *Courtesy of Alex Turco.*

already rewritten DePauw's record book for rushing yards in a game, season and career. His day didn't end until he carried the ball forty-five times and caught seven passes for 278 total yards. "I went balls to the wall in every game I went into," Marks said. "I didn't really approach that game differently besides the fact that I knew it was my last game. I feel like I gave my all for every game in general. I don't know. I had a lot of yards and played pretty well that day, so maybe I had a little bit more enthusiasm. I'm not sure exactly."

Wabash's defense didn't seem to figure out exactly how to stop Marks either. Once again with his team trailing, Marks carried the Tiger offense to start the third quarter. "It was the Jeremiah Marks show," said freshman

DePauw kicker Jordan Havercamp attempts an extra point during the 2007 Monon Bell Classic. Havercamp would later hit a forty-seven-yard field goal with time expiring to win the game. *Courtesy of Alex Turco.*

wide receiver Alex Koors. Six of the first seven plays were runs by Marks, totaling just twenty-one yards. Then he hit Wabash with a big play. Spud Dick dropped back on third-and-fifteen and, instead of throwing deep, dished a shovel pass to Marks at the line of scrimmage. The senior running back started down the middle of the field before cutting left behind a couple of blocks from his wide receivers and beat all Little Giant defenders in a race to the end zone.

A shovel pass was a twist employed by Matt Walker and offensive coordinator Dustin Ward to get Marks the ball in different ways. For an offense that used Marks repeatedly on power running plays up the middle, it was almost a trick play. "That play was awesome. We used it a couple times during the season, but we didn't overuse it," Marks said. "I loved that play. Everybody clears out, and all I had to do was run over a safety or a corner and I'm good."

The game was set to be tied, but kicking issues prevented DePauw from evening the score. Havercamp was unable to knock his third extra point of the season through the uprights.

Somehow, Wabash managed to hold onto a lead despite a defensive performance that disappointed captain linebacker Adi Pynenberg. "Defensively, it was not a sharp game for us," he said. "We really were in a holding-on-for-dear-life type of feeling. We did not feel like we were dictating the pace at all, and we were just kinda relying on our offensive guys to bail us out time and time again."

The Wabash defense did have one more important stop left in it. After the Little Giant offense was forced to punt, DePauw's offense drove into Wabash territory looking to take its first lead of the game. Faced with a third-and-seven, Dick once again looked for Mulligan, who had already caught nine passes in the game, but the pass fell incomplete. With a stable kicking game, Walker would have elected to kick a field goal with the ball on the Wabash twenty-yard line on fourth-and-seven, but both kickers already showed shaky legs. A fourth-down pass attempt by Dick failed, and Pynenberg and the Wabash defense gave the ball to quarterback Matt Hudson with a little bit of momentum.

Wabash picked up a first down in three plays on consecutive runs by running back Evan Sobecki and a completion from Hudson to Brock Graham. Then, with the ball at his own thirty-five-yard line, Hudson struck deep once again. He lofted a pass down the middle of the field to wide receiver Bart Banach, who caught the ball ahead of a trailing DePauw defender and sprinted the final thirty yards for a touchdown. The following extra point gave Wabash a 21–13 lead with fifty-one seconds left in the third quarter.

In desperate need of a score, the DePauw offense sputtered to start the fourth quarter and gave the ball back to Wabash after a three-and-out. Another score for Wabash could put the game out of reach, and the

Sophomore quarterback Matt Hudson throws a pass for Wabash during the 2007 Monon Bell Classic. Hudson lost his first two starts against DePauw before winning as a senior in 2009. *Courtesy of Alex Turco.*

DePauw quarterback Spud Dick looks to throw a pass during the 2007 Monon Bell Classic. Dick completed twenty-eight of his thirty-five pass attempts for three hundred yards and three touchdowns in a 24–21 victory. *Courtesy of Alex Turco.*

Little Giants were on the move into DePauw territory after three straight completions by Hudson. But the next set of three plays brought two incompletions, and the Little Giants were set to punt.

The miscue on third down still haunts Hudson. Needing five yards for a first down, Hudson found Mike Russell open on the Wabash sideline past the first-down marker. Rolling left, Hudson's imperfect pass forced Russell to fall to the ground to make the grab. Russell caught the pass, but a referee ruled him out of bounds. "The referee comes up and just starts waving his hands above his head as if to signal to stop the clock and a first down, but after doing that for about a half a second, he went and signaled incomplete," Hudson said. "As far as I could tell, he did get his foot in."

Replays showed that Russell may have completed the catch inbounds, but Wabash would have to punt and rely on its defense to hold onto the lead.

DePauw head coach Matt Walker and offensive coordinator Dustin Ward never strayed from the game plan. Their offense continued to run the ball and look for short passes, even with the time in the fourth quarter ticking away. The Tigers needed to sustain a drive, and fourth-down conversions became a necessity. The players called on to make those plays weren't new. DePauw wasn't going to be able to win without the legs of Jeremiah Marks, the hands of Bryan Mulligan and the arm of Spud Dick. Helped by consistent blocking from the offensive line, the Tigers scratched for the necessary yardage.

With slightly less than eleven minutes left in the game, the DePauw drive started at its own seventeen-yard line. A nineteen-yard Mulligan reception on first down brought confidence, but the three short plays left the Tigers with fourth-and-one. Dick moved the chains with a three-yard run and then once again hit Mulligan for nineteen yards on first down. The Tigers moved deeper into Wabash territory when another fourth down greeted them at the twenty-seven-yard line. A five-yard completion to Mulligan allowed the offense to remain on the field. Three plays later, the Tigers had the ball first-and-goal on the nine-yard line. Marks was stuffed on a run up the middle on first down, so DePauw decided to try something different. On second down, Dick dropped back and flipped a shovel pass to Marks, the same play that had scored earlier, and Marks found a crease behind his blockers to dive into the end zone. An unconventional play for the DePauw offense found pay dirt twice.

"It takes a certain amount of timing to make it look like a pass to get the defensive ends up the field, and then it's a left-handed pass for me," Dick said. "That took a little bit of getting used to. We were certainly surprised that we scored two touchdowns on it. It was certainly a surprise that it worked that well."

In order to tie the game with three minutes and thirty-seven seconds left, the Tigers needed a two-point conversion. Fortunately for them, they had practiced one all week. Dick still remembers the play call: Explode to Right Hap 31 Net. The play required freshman wide receiver Alex Koors to start on the left side of the offense, motion to the other side and settle down behind the line of scrimmage while other receivers worked to get open in the end zone. "We ran that play so many times during practice. All week, all year, my entire four years, Coach Ward was anal about having a two-point play ready in case we needed it," Koors said. "We ran that play so many times throughout that week, and I don't think I got the ball one time."

This time he was needed. Dick scanned the end zone for his other targets, but the two receivers on the right side were covered. Dick's initial look to those receivers sucked the defense with them toward the middle of the field. That left Koors wide open at the five-yard line just outside the numbers on the field.

"I wanted to make a hand gesture, maybe yell or something like that toward Spud, because I was open," Koors said. "But at the same point in time, you do that and then somebody sees you there. Luckily he went through all his reads and hit me."

Koors caught the ball in stride and raced to the pylon at the goal line. He dove and reached the ball out and snuck in before diving Wabash linebacker Matt Kraft could stop his momentum. The unlikely freshman, who caught only one other pass all game long, tied the game.

WITH THE BIG-PLAY ABILITY it had already shown throughout the game, Wabash's offense still had a chance to win the game. That hope started becoming more of a reality on the fourth play of the drive when Matt Hudson hit Chad Sorenson for a nineteen-yard completion down the left sideline and moved the Little Giants to the DePauw forty. C.P. Porter then rushed for five yards on first down, and Hudson threw an incomplete pass on second down. Wabash head coach Chris Creighton brought his team to the sideline for a timeout with one minute and thirty-three seconds left.

It was time for Hudson to complete the big third-down pass that he failed to do the drive before. Once again, he threw for Mike Russell, and once again, the play ended with an incomplete pass. After the game, Hudson realized he missed a wide-open receiver on the play. But in the moment, he had to worry about fourth down. This time, Creighton let Hudson make the call. Hudson wanted to try Russell, who caught fifty passes on the season, one more time. The Monon Bell game wouldn't bring a fifty-first reception. Hudson heaved a pass deep down the right side of the field, but DePauw cornerback Jevon Pruitt forced his way in between Russell and the ball. Pruitt leaped to make the interception but pinned his team at the four-yard line. An incompletion would have given his team a decent chance of moving down the field in the final minute. Instead, the game seemed destined for overtime with DePauw ninety-six yards from the Wabash end zone and just eighty-three seconds left in the fourth quarter.

"The last thing you want to do is turn the ball over to give them a shot to score," said DePauw quarterback Spud Dick. "So I think the original intent was just to run out the clock, but with the thought that if we got a first down that we could take a shot at it."

So Dick handed the ball off to trusty Jeremiah Marks on first down, and he took the ball out to the nine-yard line. Hoping to get the ball back,

Receiver Bryan Mulligan lines up wide on DePauw's final drive in the 2007 Monon Bell Classic. Mulligan caught two passes for twenty-five yards on the drive to help set up Jordan Havercamp's game-winning field goal. *Courtesy of Alex Turco.*

Wabash took a timeout. A four-yard run on second down by Marks left the Tigers with a third-and-one and the possibility of giving the ball back to the Little Giants for a last-minute drive. Instead, Marks bounced around for an eleven-yard gain, and the Tigers were no longer in the shadow of their own goalposts. A shovel pass to Marks for no gain on first down led to a DePauw timeout with thirty-one seconds left. Marks then ripped off a fourteen-yard run to the thirty-eight-yard line. With the Tigers suddenly threatening to cross midfield, Wabash took a timeout to regroup. Without the timeout, Wabash would have been called for a penalty for too many players on the field following a substitution.

"The first couple plays were pretty conservative," Dick said. "Then we were able to hit a dig route to Mulligan that really broke it and got us nineteen yards. At that point, we realized that we really could get into field goal range with enough time." Having someone to make that field goal was a different story. But with the ball at the Wabash forty-three and thirteen seconds left, the Tigers took a timeout. They just needed a couple quick plays for a prayer. "Given what had happened earlier in the game and the last couple games, I didn't think we had a field goal kicker that could come through," Dick said. "We missed an extra point earlier in the game. I knew it couldn't hurt to get into field goal range to give him a shot."

That's exactly what Dick and the Tiger offense would do. The quarterback looked right for a six-yard completion to Mulligan, who stepped out of bounds with 8.9 seconds left on the clock. Then Dick threw to Marks, who caught the ball near the hash mark at the thirty-five-yard line. Relying on the legs that already churned out so many yards in the game, Marks broke two tackles in the open field before darting for the Wabash sideline. He lunged out of bounds at the Wabash twenty-nine with 2.4 seconds left on the clock.

Now Walker had to pick a kicker or draw upon a Hail Mary. Six years to the day from the famous game-winning catch by Wabash's Kurt Casper in 2001, a last-ditch effort before overtime was only fitting.

WHO IS JORDAN HAVERCAMP? He's the kicker Matt Walker picked to give one chance to beat Wabash. All season long, the coaching staff favored Brendan Smith, a senior who also played baseball for Walker at DePauw. Walker decided to give Havercamp a chance, with Smith having missed nine of his fourteen field goal attempts throughout the season.

Still, many didn't know the answer to the question—even Walker. "Embarrassingly, I didn't know much about him," Walker said. "I was getting to know him like any other new player. Especially with those kickers and punters, you're just not around them as much."

Maybe a fellow player would know him better. "Honestly, I can't say I had said more than a couple words to him," Marks said. "He was a really quiet

DePauw celebrates with the Monon Bell after Jordan Havercamp's game-winning field goal in 2007. *Courtesy of Alex Turco.*

kid. There had been punters and kickers in the past that I was friends with and who I would talk to all the time. But he was a younger kid and pretty quiet, so I never really talked to him before."

How about fellow first-year player Alex Koors? "I knew nothing about Jordan Havercamp," Koors said. "I didn't know what his leg was like. I just knew he wore that hideous jersey. I think if he untucked it, it would have gone down to his knees. I knew nothing about him."

Even the announcers of the HDNet television broadcast were left with little detail on the identity of DePauw's kicker. Throughout the game, Joe Emmick, a 1992 Wabash grad, and Rob Doyle, a Monon Bell–winning quarterback for DePauw in 1981, joked throughout the second half that the game wouldn't be decided by a field goal from either team.

To Havercamp, the answer was simple. He was the guy that should have been kicking all season long. Each week, he'd compete with the rest of the kickers in competition and come away thinking he had the better leg. But the coaching staff hadn't put its faith behind Havercamp. That changed when Walker gave him the chance to win the game. Thousands would soon know exactly who Jordan Havercamp was.

Out trotted Havercamp with holder Brad Paus, and the two set up for the kick on the right hash mark at the thirty-seven-yard line. There stood Havercamp near the forty, a scrawny six-feet and 170 pounds, wearing a different jersey than most of the team. He wore number fifty-two, which was also worn by junior defensive lineman Grant Wright, so Havercamp's jersey was an older version, with "DEPAUW" in larger white letters across the chest and white paw prints lower on the sleeves rather than on the shoulders.

The snap came with 2.4 seconds left. Paus set the ball down, and Havercamp gave it a whack. "Right when I kicked it, I knew it was long enough and I knew it was high enough," Havercamp said. "From my angle—I had the perfect angle—I could tell it was going in. I had the right line. I was celebrating."

Shortly after the ball left the ground, Havercamp jumped up with arms raised to signal a good field goal. The ball remained true to Havercamp and sailed through the uprights with at least five yards to spare. DePauw beat Wabash 23–21.

DePauw players piled on Havercamp while the Tiger faithful flooded the field in celebration. After what seemed like ages to the Wabash players, DePauw collected itself and lined up for the postgame handshakes before claiming the Monon Bell.

A GAME LIKE THAT lasts with players and coaches. The victors remember the joy of the celebration, and the losers take pain in every mistake that led to the loss. Chris Creighton, who left Wabash following the 2007 season, still takes the blame for his team's loss. "I failed to lead our team that game," Creighton said. That day, Creighton preached to his team about being tough-nosed. He even wore a bandage across his nose to symbolize the team's toughness. The motivation didn't translate onto the field. "On that day, they were tougher than we were," he said. "I failed to get our team to be the hardest-nosed team on that day. And that's why we lost. We got beat. They wanted it more than we did, and they played harder. It's hard to say that to a Wabash team. I could count on maybe two fingers how many times that happened in my seven years there."

Hudson, who finished the game with twenty-one completions for 322 yards, still looks at those two incomplete passes on critical third downs. "In the grand scheme of the game, little plays like that don't seem like they would be that big of a deal, but obviously they did end up being a big deal. Overall, we just didn't play our best game that day," Hudson said. "I think anybody who was on the team would tell you that. We felt like we would have beaten that team probably seven or eight times out of ten. We didn't play our best, and it's one that we'll always look back on and regret."

Above: Wabash's Allen Athletics and Recreation Center sits void of the Monon Bell the day of the 2008 Monon Bell Classic. *Courtesy of Alex Turco.*

Left: DePauw student Brad Hilbrich rings the Monon Bell on DePauw's sideline during the 2009 matchup between the Tigers and Little Giants. Wabash won the game 32–19 in Blackstock Stadium to take the Bell back to Crawfordsville. *Courtesy of Alex Turco.*

A DePauw helmet is raised to the sky during the 2009 Monon Bell Classic. *Courtesy of Alex Turco.*

DePauw's empty sideline awaiting the 2009 Monon Bell Classic at Blackstock Stadium. *Courtesy of Alex Turco.*

Television cameras sit atop the press box at Blackstock Stadium waiting to capture the 2009 Monon Bell Classic. *Courtesy of Alex Turco.*

Wabash quarterback Matt Hudson refused to lose his final Monon Bell Classic in 2009. Faced with a fourth-and-one on Wabash's own seventeen-yard line, Hudson told Little Giant head coach Erik Raeburn, "I will not fail you, Coach." Hudson gained the yardage needed on a quarterback sneak and allowed the Little Giants to hold on to a 32–19 victory. *Courtesy of Tom Runge.*

Linebacker Bryan Watson celebrates a Wabash victory in the 2009 Monon Bell Classic. Watson totaled four tackles and a forced fumble in the win. *Courtesy of Alex Turco.*

Wabash fans celebrate a score in the 2009 Monon Bell Classic at Blackstock Stadium. *Courtesy of Alex Turco.*

To this day, Adi Pynenberg doesn't like to return to Blackstock Stadium. Cheering on Wabash Little Giants trying to do what he couldn't as a senior is the only thing that brings him back. "It sucks. I hate being in their stadium. Their stadium is not fun to watch football games in," Pynenberg said. "My wife and I haven't missed one Bell game since I graduated and got done coaching there. We've been to that game more than homecoming or any of the other games combined. We don't like going to Blackstock, but we do to root everybody on."

Wabash has won the two games in Blackstock Stadium since, but every other November, the memory of Havercamp's kick still hangs in the Greencastle air.

Appendix I

THE BALLAD OF THE MONON BELL

Long before the cannonball traveled through her towns
The state of Indiana owned the jewel of the crown
The train, they called the Monon, the stories they still tell
The Cavemen and the Tigers playing for her bell
It rode like a masthead on engine ninety-nine
Crawfordsville to Greencastle, then further down the line
The Cavemen came from Wabash, the Tigers from DePauw
Since eighteen-ninety they have played the last game ev'ry fall
Many years they played for pride, oh the stories they could tell
Then in thirty-two the Monon train gave up her precious bell
They said, "Here take this symbol of smoke and fire and grit
And give it to the winner, a symbol not to quit."
Ring the Bell for Wabash, ring for old DePauw
Ring the bell for victory in the last game ev'ry fall
Ring the Bell for Wabash, ring for old DePauw
Ring the bell for victory in the last game ev'ry fall
Suddenly the boys of autumn had fire in their eyes
Blood and spit, but never quit, fighting for the prize

The medal to the victor, the symbol to the school
Wabash and DePauw became a yearly duel
Ring the Bell for Wabash, ring for old DePauw
Ring the bell for victory in the last game ev'ry fall
Ring the Bell for Wabash, ring for old DePauw
Ring the bell for victory in the last game ev'ry fall
Now history has recorded the players and their games
And to this day they still play for the Bell in Monon's name
Those who've gone before return each November day
Swapping stories and the legends for those who did not play
Ring the Bell for Wabash, ring for old DePauw
Ring the bell for victory in the last game ev'ry fall
Ring the Bell for Wabash, ring for old DePauw
Ring the bell for victory in the last game ev'ry fall

Appendix II
MONON BELL RESULTS

DATE	SITE	WINNER	SCORE	RECORD
11/22/1890	Crawfordsville	DePauw	34–5	D, 1–0
11/21/1891	Greencastle	DePauw	1–0 (For)	D, 2–0
11/5/1892	Greencastle	DePauw	42–4	D, 3–0
11/11/1893	Crawfordsville	DePauw	48–34	D, 4–0
10/20/1894	Greencastle	Wabash	16–4	D, 4–1
10/19/1895	Crawfordsville	Wabash	6–0	D, 4–2
10/31/1896	Greencastle	DePauw	20–0	D, 5–2
10/6/1900	Crawfordsville	Wabash	6–0	D, 5–3
11/12/1900	Greencastle	DePauw	26–11	D, 6–3
11/11/1901	Greencastle	DePauw	31–2	D, 7–3
11/18/1901	Crawfordsville	DePauw	35–5	D, 8–3
11/21/1903	Crawfordsville	Wabash	10–0	D, 8–4
11/23/1905	Crawfordsville	Wabash	52–0	D, 8–5
11/17/1906	Greencastle	Wabash	7–0	D, 8–6
11/4/1907	Crawfordsville	Wabash	11–4	D, 8–7
11/20/1908	Crawfordsville	Wabash	12–0	Tied, 8–8

DATE	SITE	WINNER	SCORE	RECORD
10/9/1909	Greencastle	Tie	0–0	Tied, 8–8–1
10/13/1911	Crawfordsville	Tie	0–0	Tied, 8–8–2
10/12/1912	Greencastle	Wabash	62–0	W, 9–8–2
10/20/1913	Crawfordsville	DePauw	7–0	Tied, 9–9–2
11/16/1914	Greencastle	DePauw	3–0	D, 10–9–2
11/20/1915	Crawfordsville	Wabash	34–0	Tied, 10–10–2
11/11/1916	Indianapolis	Wabash	26–13	W, 11–10–2
11/10/1917	Indianapolis	DePauw	7–0	Tied, 11–11–2
11/23/1918	Crawfordsville	DePauw	28–6	D, 12–11–2
11/8/1919	Indianapolis	Tie	0–0	D, 12–11–3
11/20/1920	Indianapolis	DePauw	3–0	D, 13–11–3
11/19/1921	Indianapolis	Wabash	22–0	D, 13–12–3
11/25/1922	Indianapolis	Wabash	30–0	Tied, 13–13–3
11/24/1923	Crawfordsville	Wabash	17–0	W, 14–13–3
11/22/1924	Greencastle	Wabash	21–0	W, 15–13–3
11/21/1925	Crawfordsville	Wabash	22–0	W, 16–13–3
11/20/1926	Greencastle	Wabash	6–0	W, 17–13–3
11/19/1927	Crawfordsville	Wabash	13–7	W, 18–13–3
11/24/1928	Greencastle	DePauw	20–12	W, 18–14–3
11/23/1929	Crawfordsville	Wabash	8–7	W, 19–14–3
11/22/1930	Greencastle	DePauw	7–6	W, 19–15–3
11/21/1931	Crawfordsville	DePauw	13–7	W, 19–16–3
11/19/1932	Greencastle	Tie	0–0	W, 19–16–4
11/18/1933	Crawfordsville	DePauw	14–0	W, 19–17–4
11/17/1934	Greencastle	Wabash	7–6	W, 20–17–4
11/16/1935	Greencastle	Tie	0–0	W, 20–17–5
11/14/1936	Greencastle	Wabash	19–0	W, 21–17–5
11/14/1937	Crawfordsville	DePauw	32–0	W, 21–18–5
11/12/1938	Greencastle	DePauw	7–0	W, 21–19–5

DATE	SITE	WINNER	SCORE	RECORD
11/18/1939	Crawfordsville	DePauw	7–0	W, 21–20–5
11/16/1940	Greencastle	Wabash	17–13	W, 22–20–5
11/15/1941	Crawfordsville	Wabash	27–9	W, 23–20–5
11/14/1942	Greencastle	DePauw	6–3	W, 23–21–5
10/16/1943	Greencastle	DePauw	33–0	W, 23–22–5
10/21/1944	Crawfordsville	Wabash	14–7	W, 24–22–5
9/22/1945	Greencastle	DePauw	13–7	W, 24–23–5
11/16/1946	Crawfordsville	Wabash	26–0	W, 25–23–5
11/15/1947	Greencastle	Wabash	27–7	W, 26–23–5
11/13/1948	Crawfordsville	DePauw	8–0	W, 26–24–5
11/12/1949	Greencastle	Wabash	25–21	W, 27–24–5
11/18/1950	Crawfordsville	Wabash	34–20	W, 28–24–5
11/17/1951	Greencastle	Wabash	41–12	W, 29–24–5
11/15/1952	Crawfordsville	Wabash	47–0	W, 30–24–5
11/14/1953	Greencastle	Wabash	41–0	W, 31–24–5
11/13/1954	Crawfordsville	Wabash	28–0	W, 32–24–5
11/12/1955	Greencastle	DePauw	23–20	W, 32–25–5
11/17/1956	Crawfordsville	Tie	7–7	W, 32–25–6
11/16/1957	Greencastle	DePauw	37–6	W, 32–26–6
11/15/1958	Crawfordsville	DePauw	24–8	W, 32–27–6
11/14/1959	Greencastle	Tie	6–6	W, 32–27–7
11/12/1960	Crawfordsville	DePauw	14–13	W, 32–28–7
11/18/1961	Greencastle	DePauw	20–7	W, 32–29–7
11/17/1962	Crawfordsville	DePauw	13–10	W, 32–30–7
11/16/1963	Greencastle	DePauw	17–0	W, 32–31–7
11/14/1964	Crawfordsville	DePauw	22–21	Tied, 32–32–7
11/13/1965	Greencastle	Wabash	16–6	W, 33–32–7
11/12/1966	Crawfordsville	DePauw	9–7	Tied, 33–33–7
11/11/1967	Greencastle	Wabash	7–0	W, 34–33–7

DATE	SITE	WINNER	SCORE	RECORD
11/16/1968	Crawfordsville	DePauw	18–7	Tied, 34–34–7
11/15/1969	Greencastle	DePauw	17–7	D, 35–34–7
11/7/1970	Crawfordsville	DePauw	14–13	D, 36–34–7
11/13/1971	Greencastle	Wabash	16–7	D, 36–35–7
11/11/1972	Crawfordsville	Wabash	20–14	Tied, 36–36–7
11/10/1973	Greencastle	DePauw	28–21	D, 37–36–7
11/16/1974	Crawfordsville	DePauw	15–12	D, 38–36–7
11/15/1975	Greencastle	DePauw	14–8	D, 39–36–7
11/13/1976	Crawfordsville	Wabash	14–7	D, 39–37–7
11/12/1977	Greencastle	Wabash	30–6	D, 39–38–7
11/11/1978	Crawfordsville	Wabash	11–3	Tied, 39–39–7
11/10/1979	Greencastle	Wabash	16–13	W, 40–39–7
11/8/1980	Crawfordsville	Tie	22–22	W, 40–39–8
11/14/1981	Greencastle	DePauw	21–14	Tied, 40–40–8
11/13/1982	Crawfordsville	Wabash	31–6	W, 41–40–8
11/12/1983	Greencastle	DePauw	16–10	Tied, 41–41–8
11/10/1984	Crawfordsville	Wabash	41–26	W, 42–41–8
11/9/1985	Greencastle	Wabash	28–8	W, 43–41–8
11/8/1986	Crawfordsville	Wabash	24–23	W, 44–41–8
11/14/1987	Greencastle	DePauw	33–11	W, 44–42–8
11/12/1988	Crawfordsville	DePauw	24–14	W, 44–43–8
11/11/1989	Greencastle	DePauw	41–14	Tied, 44–44–8
11/10/1990	Crawfordsville	DePauw	20–13	D, 45–44–8
11/16/1991	Greencastle	Wabash	23–18	Tied, 45–45–8
11/14/1992	Crawfordsville	Tie	17–17	Tied, 45–45–9
11/13/1993	Greencastle	Wabash	40–26	W, 46–45–9
11/12/1994	Crawfordsville	Wabash	28–24	W, 47–45–9
11/11/1995	Greencastle	Wabash	7–2	W, 48–45–9

DATE	SITE	WINNER	SCORE	RECORD
11/16/1996	Crawfordsville	DePauw	31–13	W, 48–46–9
11/15/1997	Greencastle	DePauw	14–7	W, 48–47–9
11/14/1998	Crawfordsville	DePauw	42–7	Tied, 48–48–9
11/13/1999	Greencastle	DePauw	21–7	D, 49–48–9
11/11/2000	Crawfordsville	DePauw	27–17	D, 50–48–9
11/10/2001	Greencastle	Wabash	27–21	D, 50–49–9
11/16/2002	Crawfordsville	Wabash	35–7	Tied, 50–50–9
11/15/2003	Greencastle	Wabash	37–20	W, 51–50–9
11/13/2004	Crawfordsville	DePauw	14–7	Tied, 51–51–9
11/12/2005	Greencastle	Wabash	17–14	W, 52–51–9
11/11/2006	Crawfordsville	Wabash	23–20	W, 53–51–9
11/10/2007	Greencastle	DePauw	24–21	W, 53–52–9
11/15/2008	Crawfordsville	DePauw	36–14	Tied, 53–53–9
11/14/2009	Greencastle	Wabash	32–19	W, 54–53–9
11/13/2010	Crawfordsville	Wabash	47–0	W, 55–53–9
11/12/2011	Greencastle	Wabash	45–7	W, 56–53–9
11/10/2012	Crawfordsville	Wabash	23–0	W, 57–53–9

ABOUT THE AUTHOR

Tyler James has spent his falls on and around football fields since early childhood. Michigan-born and Indiana-raised, he grew to love the game as a coach's kid, a high school football player and, now, a newspaper reporter. A 2011 graduate of DePauw University, he currently works as a staff writer for the *South Bend Tribune* covering Notre Dame football recruiting year-round.

Visit us at
www.historypress.net
···
This title is also available as an e-book